PASSION
TRANSLATION

THE PASSIONATE LIFE BIBLE STUDY SERIES

12-LESSON STUDY GUIDE

THE BOOK OF
GALATIANS

HEAVEN'S FREEDOM

BroadStreet
PUBLISHING

BroadStreet Publishing® Group, LLC
Savage, Minnesota, USA
BroadStreetPublishing.com

TPT: The Book of Galatians: 12-Lesson Study Guide
Copyright © 2023 BroadStreet Publishing Group

9781424566266 (softcover)
9781424566273 (e-book)

Stock or custom editions of BroadStreet Publishing titles may be purchased in bulk for educational, business, ministry, fundraising, or sales promotional use. For information, please email orders@ broadstreetpublishing.com.

General editor: Brian Simmons
Managing editor: William D. Watkins
Writer: Matthew A. Boardwell

Design and typesetting by Garborg Design Works | garborgdesign.com

Printed in China

23 24 25 26 27 5 4 3 2 1

Contents

From God's Heart to Yours 4

Why I Love the Book of Galatians 9

Lesson 1   The Writer, the Readers, the Problem 11

Lesson 2   Sent Out and Welcomed In 30

Lesson 3   Peter, Paul, and the Rest of Us 51

Lesson 4   How to Arrive at Righteousness 71

Lesson 5   What the Law Did for Us 88

Lesson 6   All God's Children 105

Lesson 7   Losing Ground 119

Lesson 8   Who's Your Mama? 130

Lesson 9   Fragile Freedom 148

Lesson 10   The Fruit Fight 161

Lesson 11   The Burdens We Bear 178

Lesson 12   Identifying with the Cross 194

Appendix   Answer Key to Lesson 3 Timeline 208

Endnotes   211

From God's Heart to Yours

"God is love," says the apostle John, and "Everyone who loves is fathered by God and experiences an intimate knowledge of him" (1 John 4:7). The life of a Christ-follower is, at its core, a life of love—God's love of us, our love of him, and our love of others and ourselves because of God's love for us.

And this divine love is reliable, trustworthy, unconditional, other-centered, majestic, forgiving, redemptive, patient, kind, and more precious than anything else we can ever receive or give. It characterizes each person of the Trinity—Father, Son, and Holy Spirit—and so is as limitless as they are. They love one another with this eternal love, and they reach beyond themselves to us, created in their image with this love.

How do we know such incredible truths? Through the primary source of all else we know about the one God—his Word, the Bible. Of course, God reveals who he is through other sources as well, such as the natural world, miracles, our inner life, our relationships (especially with him), those who minister on his behalf, and those who proclaim him to us and others. But the fullest and most comprehensive revelation we have of God and from him is what he has given us in the thirty-nine books of the Hebrew Scriptures (the Old Testament) and the twenty-seven books of the Christian Scriptures (the New Testament). Together, these sixty-six books present a compelling and telling portrait of God and his dealings with us.

It is these Scriptures that *The Passionate Life Bible Study Series* is all about. Through these study guides, we—the editors and writers of this series—seek to provide you with a unique and welcoming opportunity to delve more deeply into God's precious Word, encountering there his loving heart for you and all the others he loves. God wants you to know him more deeply, to love him more devoutly, and to share his heart with others more frequently and freely. To accomplish this, we have based this study guide series on The Passion Translation of the Bible, which strives to "reintroduce the passion and fire of the Bible to the English reader. It doesn't merely convey the literal meaning of words. It expresses God's passion for people and his world by translating the original, life-changing message of God's Word for modern readers." It has been created to "kindle in you a burning desire to know the heart of God, while impacting the church for years to come."[1]

In each study guide, you will find an introduction to the Bible book it covers. There you will gain information about that Bible book's authorship, date of composition, first recipients, setting, purpose, central message, and key themes. Each lesson following the introduction will take a portion of that Bible book and walk you through it so you will learn its content better while experiencing and applying God's heart for your own life and encountering ways you can share his heart with others. Along the way, you will come across a number of features we have created that provide opportunities for more life application and growth in biblical understanding.

 ## Experience God's Heart

This feature focuses questions on personal application. It will help you live out God's Word and to bring the Bible into your world in fresh, exciting, and relevant ways.

 ## Share God's Heart

This feature will help you grow in your ability to share with other people what you learn and apply in a given lesson. It provides guidance on using the lesson to grow closer to others and to enrich your fellowship with others. It also points the way to enabling you to better listen to the stories of others so you can bridge the biblical story with their stories.

The Backstory

This feature provides ancient historical and cultural background that illuminates Bible passages and teachings. It deals with then-pertinent religious groups, communities, leaders, disputes, business trades, travel routes, customs, nations, political factions, ancient measurements and currency...in short, anything historical or cultural that will help you better understand what Scripture says and means.

Word Wealth

This feature provides definitions for and other illuminating information about key terms, names, and concepts, and how different ancient languages have influenced the biblical text. It also provides insight into the different literary forms in the Bible, such as prophecy, poetry, narrative history, parables, and letters, and how knowing the form of a text can help you better interpret and apply it. Finally, this feature highlights the most significant passages in a Bible book. You may be encouraged to memorize these verses or keep them before you in some way so you can actively hide God's Word in your heart.

Digging Deeper

This feature explains the theological significance of a text or the controversial issues that arise and mentions resources you can use to help you arrive at your own conclusions. Another way to dig deeper into the Word is by looking into the life of a biblical character or another person from church history, showing how that man or woman incarnated a biblical truth or passage. For instance, Jonathan Edwards was well known for his missions work among native American Indians and for his intellectual prowess in articulating the Christian faith, Florence Nightingale for the reforms she brought about in healthcare, Irenaeus for his fight against heresy, Billy Graham for his work in evangelism, Moses for the strength God gave him to lead the Hebrews and receive and communicate the law, and Deborah for her work as a judge in Israel. This feature introduces to you figures from the past who model what it looks like to experience God's heart and share his heart with others.

The Extra Mile

While The Passion Translation's notes are extensive, sometimes students of Scripture like to explore more on their own. In this feature, we provide you with opportunities to glean more information from a Bible dictionary, a Bible encyclopedia, a reliable Bible online tool, another ancient text, and the like. Here you will learn how you can go the extra mile on a Bible lesson. And not just in study either. Reflection, prayer, discussion, and applying a passage in new ways provide even more opportunities to go the extra mile. Here you will find questions to answer and applications to make that will require more time and energy from you—if and when you have them to give.

As you can see above, each of these features has a corresponding icon so you can quickly and easily identify them.

You will find other helps and guidance through the lessons of these study guides, including thoughtful questions, application suggestions, and spaces for you to record your own reflections, answers, and action steps. Of course, you can also write in your own journal, notebook, computer document, or other resource, but we have provided you with space for your convenience.

Also, each lesson will direct you toward the introductory material and numerous notes provided in The Passion Translation. There each Bible book contains a number of aids supplied to help you better grasp God's words and his incredible love, power, knowledge, plans, and so much more. We want you to get the most out of your Bible study, especially using it to draw you closer to the One who loves you most.

Finally, at the end of each lesson you'll find a section called "Talking It Out." This contains questions and exercises for application that you can share, answer, and apply with your spouse, a friend, a coworker, a Bible study group, or any other individuals or groups who would like to walk with you through this material. As Christians, we gather together to serve, study, worship, sing, evangelize, and a host of other activities. We grow together, not just on our own. This section will give you ample opportunities to engage others with some of the content of each lesson so you can work it out in community.

We offer all of this to support you in becoming an even more faithful and loving disciple of Jesus Christ. A disciple in the ancient world was a student of her teacher, a follower of his master. Students study, and followers follow. Jesus' disciples are to sit at his feet and listen and learn and then do what he tells them and shows them to do. We have created *The Passionate Life Bible Study Series* to help you do what a disciple of Jesus is called to do.

So go.

Read God's words.

Hear what he has to say in them and through them.

Meditate on them.

Hide them in your heart.

Display their truths in your life.

Share their truths with others.

Let them ignite Jesus' passion and light in all you say and do.

Use them to help you fulfill what Jesus called his disciples to do: "Now wherever you go, make disciples of all nations, baptizing them in the name of the Father, the Son, and the Holy Spirit. And teach them to faithfully follow all that I have commanded you. And never forget that I am with you every day, even to the completion of this age" (Matthew 28:19–20).

And through all of this, let Jesus' love nourish your heart and allow that love to overflow into your relationships with others (John 15:9–13). For it was for love that Jesus came, served, died, rose from the dead, and ascended into heaven. This love he gives us. And this love he wants us to pass along to others.

Why I Love the Book of Galatians

A mighty wave of freedom is sweeping over the church today. It is a freedom purchased for us at the cross of Jesus. His blood, his nails, and his suffering become a doorway into true spiritual freedom. I love the book of Galatians because it presents to me and to every other believer the wonderful, joyous freedom of Christ. He has set us free from death, sin, vanity, and demonic powers. Our soul-freedom cannot be made more complete or perfect. We cannot better what Christ has done for us. Caution: reading Galatians may make you dance with joy!

Paul didn't wait long after his conversion before he realized how the churches of Galatia needed this freedom. They had been entangled with their past relationship with the law and the traditions of their ancestors. They needed the wise words of Paul to show them how they could step into the full freedom of the gospel. It excites me to know that when I read Galatians, I may be reading the first book Paul wrote.

I love Galatians because it also gives me a glimpse into the life and ministry of the apostle Paul himself. Paul was twice blinded: once to the truth of the gospel of Jesus Christ and then blinded again by the revelation that he had been persecuting Jesus, not just his followers. Paul gives us other details in Galatians that we read nowhere else in his writings. For example, he went into the desert to meet with God after his conversion. He may have even journeyed to Mount Sinai—the very place where Moses gave the law—to learn from God firsthand about heaven's freedom in the gospel.

The book of Galatians is a gospel presentation of God's endless grace. This grace-filled gospel brings heaven's freedom into our lives—freedom to live for God and serve one another, as well as freedom from religious bondage. We can thank God today that Paul's gospel is still being preached and heaven's freedom is available to every believer. We are free to soar even higher than keeping religious laws; we have a grace-righteousness that places us at the right hand of the throne of God, not as servants, but as sons and daughters of the Most High. That's why I love this book.

But perhaps my favorite theme in Galatians is the life of the Spirit. The fruit of the Holy Spirit is that glorious relationship we can have, not with keeping rules and traditions, but with keeping in step with the Holy Spirit. He will conquer every residue of our old life, bring us into the truth of the gospel, and produce the fruit of Christ's life in us. The Holy Spirit wants to meet you and give you a taste of heaven's freedom as you read through this study guide. Let him speak to you. Let him lead you into the deeper truth of the glorious freedom Christ has given to us.

LESSON 1

The Writer, the Readers, the Problem

(Galatians 1:1–10)

"Stop!"

"Don't take another step!"

"Look out!"

Reading those words, you can immediately think of situations where they might apply. Situations with genuine imminent danger, maybe even life-threatening circumstances. Situations that demand sharp, maybe even harsh, confrontation, certainly not nuance or politeness. A mother calling out to her young children as they run toward a busy street. A police officer waving down a car due to a serious road hazard ahead. A scout leader guiding his troop along a flooded riverbank. A driver-training instructor who sees danger before the student does.

Or maybe these could be the words of an apostle, firing off a sternly worded warning to new churches full of new Christians. That's Paul's letter to the Galatians.

As we embark on a study of Galatians, we must note the urgency of its message. When Paul penned it, there was no time for pleasantries or comfort. The fledgling churches of Galatia were facing a spiritual emergency, and the outcome would be eternal. Paul wrote to confront, to warn, and to correct these new Christians who were naively embracing false teaching that threatened to corrupt the pure message of Jesus' good news. These dangerous ideas were already swaying the members of the new church, so it appeared to Paul that the infant Christian movement in Galatia was being smothered in its cradle.

Through our study of Galatians, we will learn what this false teaching was, why it was so deadly, and how Christians must remain vigilant against it today. In doing so, we will also see clearly the pure, uncorrupted good news for everyone. We will relish its declaration of radical grace for both personal salvation and practical, godly living.

Who Wrote This Letter?

- *Who penned the letter to the Galatians, and how did he describe himself (Galatians 1:1)?*

- *Where are Paul's intended readers? How does he describe them (v. 2)?*

- *In his initial greeting, he blesses his readers, hoping they will experience what two spiritual realities?*

In the New Testament, only a small subset of the Christian community received the title of apostle. In the broadest sense, it means anyone who is sent out with a message. In the narrower, more common biblical sense, it refers to the hand-picked men whom Jesus himself sent out to disciple the nations. As we will see, Paul believed he was this type of apostle. Here, Paul made it clear what he meant when he told us who was doing his sending.

- *Paul insists that his apostleship is from Jesus himself and not merely from another well-respected Christian. Why do you think this is important to establish from the start? What difference might it make to Paul's readers?*

There was no one better to write this passionate defense of the true gospel than the apostle Paul. Because of his religious background, he once promoted some of the same anti-gospel ideas. As a devout Jew, he was a life-long student of the Old Testament (Acts 22:3). He had been a member of the Pharisees, an especially disciplined order of Jews who championed strict adherence to the law of Moses (Philippians 3:5–6).

When some Jews began to preach the good news about Jesus rising from the dead and God's free gift of salvation through him, the pre-converted Paul was furious. He was convinced that this new teaching was heresy and had to be stamped out. He persecuted these Jesus followers wherever he could find them, raiding their homes and meetings to drag them off for punishment (Acts 8:3; 22:4–5). There was no greater enemy of Jesus' message than Paul.

Then Jesus met him. That's right! The resurrected Jesus personally confronted Paul while he was on his way to persecute some more Christians in Damascus (22:6–13). From that moment on, the man who had been the unrivaled scourge of Christians became one of their chief spokesmen (9:20–22). More than that, his conversion included a calling to take the pure good news of Jesus to non-Jews too (22:14–16). Non-Jews like the Galatians.

Who Received This Letter?

Paul wrote many letters to believers to whom he had preached the good news. Sometimes he sent his letters to individuals like Titus and Philemon. Sometimes his letters went to believers in specific cities like Thessalonica or Corinth. This letter to the Galatians was for all the Christians living in the region, no matter to which local group of believers they belonged.

• *Compare Galatians 1:2 to 1:13. Why do you think Paul wrote about the churches and the church? Which is bigger, the church or the churches? What is the difference?*

 THE BACKSTORY

Galatia was a province of Rome that encompassed much of what we think of today as the Central Anatoly Peninsula of Turkey. Ankara, Turkey's modern capital, was an important city even then. It was the provincial capital located in northern Galatia. While Paul may have traveled that far north during his ministry, the named towns and villages of Galatia where he preached the gospel and strengthened the churches were all in its extreme south.

Paul's Recorded Ministry in the Region of South Galatia			
Acts Passages	**Town/ City**	**Key Events**	**Response/Results**
13:14–52			
14:1–7			
14:8–20			
14:20–23			
16:1–6			
18:23			

When Was Galatians Written?

Galatians is the first of the shorter letters in the New Testament (placed after the long ones to the Romans and Corinthians). It was almost certainly the first to be written chronologically, probably during the long period of time that Paul stayed in Antioch after his return from his first ministry tour of Galatia (Acts 14:26–28), likely sometime between AD 47 and 49.

A handful of biblical scholars think Paul may have written the letter to the Galatians later in his ministry, perhaps after his second missionary journey, but the vast majority opt for a much earlier date.[2] Among the reasons are these:

1. Paul encountered the Galatians on his first missionary journey before he ministered in the other cities that would receive his other epistles.

2. His "how quickly" comment in Galatians 1:6 indicates that he is addressing a crisis that cropped up shortly after his initial work in Galatia.

3. The issue at stake throughout the letter is the Judaizing of gentile believers (more about this shortly). This issue raged for a relatively short period of time at the beginning of gentile outreach until the apostles and other leaders in Jerusalem gave a definitive answer to the conflict at the Jerusalem Council around AD 50 (see Acts 15).

4. The letter to the Galatians never mentions that momentous council. If it had already taken place, Paul could have appealed to the decision made there. After all, all the key, well-respected authorities in the church met to consider the primary issue that Paul wrote this letter to confront. And they concluded exactly what he taught in the letter. Especially when he details his biography in Galatians 2:1–10, it defies reason that he would not even mention the council's authoritative and Spirit-led decision. While this is an argument from silence—arguments that are not typically

strong ones—failure to bring up the supporting decision of the Jerusalem council, assuming it had already occurred, is odd at best and incredulous at worst. It makes more sense to conclude that Paul didn't mention the council because it had not yet occurred. This would then place the writing of Galatians most likely in the mid to late forties.

Setting the Scene

- *Paul opened this letter by focusing the readers' attention on Jesus (Galatians 1:1–5). Jesus is Paul's sender. Jesus is distinct from ordinary men, raised from the dead, the grace- and peace-giver, the Lord, given for our sins, and our rescuer. How do these descriptions resonate with you? Which ones stand out to you?*

• *Jesus' sacrifice for sin rescued us from the present evil age and system (v. 4). What is it about this era of history and the present system that makes them evil?*

• *What among today's evils distresses or grieves you?*

• *Do you think the false teaching that Paul will confront is included in that evil?*

Why Did Paul Write to the Galatians?

Wasting no time, Paul gets right to his point. In every other letter, he includes at this point some commendation or word of encouragement for his readers. Not so with the Galatians. In a jarring turn from the "Amen" in verse 5, Paul immediately confronts the Galatians for their deadly gullibility.

- *After reading Galatians 1:6–10, write down three adjectives that describe Paul's reaction to their gospel confusion.*

- *The Galatian Christians had the pure liberating good news for only a little while, and already they were turning away from it. In doing so, they were turning away from God himself. Why do you think that deserting the good news is equivalent to deserting God?*

- *While the specifics of the false teaching aren't clear from the text yet, there is a hint. God called us to live in the grace of Christ (v. 6). What does grace mean to you? How do we live in it?*

Apparently, before the paint was even dry on the Galatians' newfound faith in Christ, other teachers had already come along offering a different message. This message was not *altogether* different. It was not so different that these new Christians would reject it out of hand. Instead, it was a perversion of the pure good news. The word "distorted" Paul used means to twist or turn. Any change to the good news he preached turns it into bad news.

We will look at this false doctrine more closely as our study unfolds. For now, suffice it to say that this small addition to the gospel is a twist that undermines it entirely. Adding law to grace does not improve grace; it erases it. Paul says this addition makes the good news no good news at all.

- *Paul had strong words for anyone who would twist the good news into bad news. What did he wish for those who taught a message contrary to his (vv. 8–9)? What if the teacher was someone they respected or even a supernatural messenger? Would Paul's assessment of them still stand?*

- *What do you think are the consequences of false teaching about eternal life?*

- *Why would Paul condemn these teachers so harshly? Why would eternal condemnation be a just penalty for them? Is it better for a single deceiver to perish or for all his victims to perish through his deception?*

If the false gospel cannot save, then all those who succumb to it are condemned. Paul's cry is that the deceiver alone would face God's righteous judgment rather than dragging all the new believers with him.

- *Paul opened his letter with a direct confrontation. Have you ever passed over pleasantries to go straight into a conflict? What were the circumstances, and how did the situation turn out?*

- *Because of the danger Paul saw in the false teaching, he chose confrontation first. He wasn't out to please people (v. 10) or approach the situation as if the threat wasn't serious. Have you ever found yourself in such a situation? How did you handle it? How were your words and actions received?*

DIGGING DEEPER

There is an old and comical Irish blessing and curse: May those who love us, love us; and those who don't love us, may God turn their hearts; and if he doesn't turn their hearts, may he turn their ankles so we'll know them by their limping.

To be sure, a turned ankle is mild compared to being condemned by God, but it is an imprecation. *Imprecation* is the biblical term for announcing a curse on someone or wishing or praying for God's punishment on someone else. Imprecations are more common in the Old Testament than in the New Testament.

Read the following Old Testament imprecations. In each of these examples, the believer witnessed injustice or cruelty and demanded that God avenge. What problem was the writer confronting? What was the curse(s) he pronounced?

OT Example	Issues	Imprecations
Deut. 27:14–26		
Psalm 35:1–8		
Psalm 55:9–15		
Psalm 58:1–11		
Psalm 69:22–28		
Psalm 109:6–20		
Psalm 140:9–11		

This is the larger biblical context for Paul's imprecation against the promoters of any false gospel. He saw the potential eternal harm that would come to anyone who was fooled to accept what was false, and he urged that God take action. In the same vein, the Protestant reformer Martin Luther instructed his followers to pray a curse on spiritual opponents: "We should pray that our enemies be converted and become our friends and, if not, that their doing and designing be bound to fail and have no success and that their persons perish rather than the Gospel and the kingdom of Christ."[3]

- *By the way, Galatians 1:8–9 are not the only imprecations in the New Testament. Read the following New Testament passages. Who is speaking? Who is spoken about? What imprecation is pronounced or demanded?*

NT Example	Speaker	Target Audience	Imprecation
Matthew 23:13–36			
Galatians 5:11–12			
James 5:1–6			
Revelation 6:9–11			

- *How do you feel about imprecations?*

- *How do biblical imprecations square with Jesus' teaching to "bless those who curse you"?*

 EXPERIENCE GOD'S HEART

- *Understanding the pure good news of Jesus is central to Paul's letter to the Galatians. That is why he begins with the resurrection and sacrifice of Christ. When did you first hear about God's rescue plan in Christ?*

- *How did you respond when you learned that Jesus' death was for your sins?*

- *What does it mean for you that God raised Jesus from the dead?*

- *Galatians begins with a scathing rebuke, and there is more to come. Have you ever needed a sharp correction? Was there anyone who loved you enough to give it? How did you respond?*

 SHARE GOD'S HEART

- *Have you ever been called on to tell the hard truth? Were you tempted to avoid the situation? Did you decide to "keep it positive" to avoid the discomfort of conflict?*

- *What are the dangers of not giving a harsh correction when one is needed?*

- *In some ways, the good news itself has a hard edge to it. The fact that a person is forever lost without the pure gospel is a difficult message for some to hear. How are you motivated to tell the indispensable truth even though it might hurt the other person to hear it?*

Talking It Out

1. The Galatian Christians were new to the Christian faith when the false teachers began to steer them wrong. Are new believers more susceptible to deception than others? Why or why not? How can local churches help new Christians stand firm in the face of false philosophies or heretical teaching?

2. From Galatians we see that the temptation to add rules to the gospel is as old as the gospel itself. Sincere religious people frequently add cultural, ritual, and moral demands to the radical grace message of Jesus. What is it about rule keeping that is so attractive to believers?

3. Have you ever had someone question your faith because you failed to live up to the religious expectations of others? If so, what was that like for you? How did it impact you?

4. Do you think the modern Christian church still puts extra-biblical obligations on new believers? If so, provide some examples.

LESSON 2

Sent Out and Welcomed In

(Galatians 1:11–2:10)

A job listing, the very one you have been hoping for, appears on a company's website. Because you have been anticipating this, you are already prepared and can apply within moments. You click on the link, enter your personal details, and then upload an important document, such as your résumé or curriculum vitae.

What is so important about this document? Why do so many job applications require one? Your résumé describes your qualifications, learning, work experience, skills, and successes. It details why you are a credible candidate for the post. It explains why the employer should take you seriously.

Again and again in Paul's ministry, he was called on to give his credentials (Acts 26:1–29; 2 Corinthians 11:16–33; 12:11–12; Philippians 3:3–6). Because of Paul's unusual message, both Jews and gentiles needed to know why they should believe him. Because of his unusual history and conversion, even fellow believers needed proof that he was legitimate (Acts 9:26–27). His personal qualifications were unique and convincing. That is why he recites them to the Galatians in our current passage.

• *Read Galatians 1:11–2:3. Summarize what Paul presents as his credentials. Given his qualifications, why can he be trusted to accurately present the gospel to others?*

• *If you had to give the credentials for why others should believe you when you speak about Jesus, what would you say? What training or experiences have given you the confidence to tell others about him?*

The Galatian believers, still young in the Lord, had two alternative messages to consider. One is uniting believing in Christ to obeying the law of Moses. With this option, faith is the start, but obedience completes our salvation. This message was brought to them confidently and persuasively enough that, within a short time after believing in Christ, they were convinced it was true.

The other option is Paul's radical grace message, that faith in Christ, independent of the law, is enough to save us. It is enough to sustain and mature us in our faith. It is enough to direct us into the good and godly life, the new and satisfying life that Jesus promised (John 10:10). Faith in Christ is enough.

While both options include Christ, only one of them can be the true gospel. If one of them is true, the other is false and perverted. How would the Galatian Christians know which teachers to believe?

- *Paul begins to answer this question in Galatians 1:11–12. What claim does Paul make here about the source of his message? Who taught him the gospel? Just as importantly, who did not teach the gospel to Paul?*

- *What authority does Paul appeal to (compare 1:11 with 1:1)? How does that authority compare to that of the false teachers?*

- *In 1:1, what title did Paul use for himself? What does it mean to have this title? The information in TPT's study note 'b' for 1:1 will be helpful here.*

We all heard the gospel from someone else. We were taught through the testimony and scriptural writings of others. We have taken classes, listened to sermons, and read articles and commentaries, all delivered by other Christians who, in turn, received the gospel from other Christians, who heard from other Christians, and so on. This supply chain goes all the way back to the earliest apostles, the ones who first followed Jesus by faith. To these, Paul was added in just a few years. And like the original twelve apostles, Paul received Jesus' gospel teaching via revelation from Jesus himself.

Paul claims he was miraculously included in this unique group of gospel authority. To prove it, he makes three claims that his opponents could not. These claims flow from his dramatic personal biography. His authority is grounded in three ways: who he has become, who sent him out, and who welcomed him in.

⏺ DIGGING DEEPER

Determining the credibility of a witness is often tricky, especially when we desire a specific outcome. Throughout biblical history, various people were called on to prove their case, like Paul did for the Galatians. Sometimes it took careful reasoning. Sometimes it took a miracle. In Paul's case, it took a little of both.

- *Read the following examples of challenges to a person's credibility. Was the credibility question resolved? How? What did the challenger eventually believe?*

  Moses before the Hebrew elders (Exodus 3:13–14; 4:1–9, 29–31)

Moses before Pharaoh (Exodus 7:8–23)

Korah, Dathan, and Abiram challenging Moses and Aaron in the desert (Numbers 16:1–35)

Aaron's priesthood challenged (Numbers 17:1–10)

Testing a prophet's credibility (Deuteronomy 18:18–22)

Two mothers seeking King Solomon's judgment (1 Kings 3:16–28)

Elijah facing the prophets of Baal (1 Kings 18:21–39)

Hananiah the prophet confronting Jeremiah (Jeremiah 28:1–17)

The scribes questioning Jesus' ability to forgive sins (Mark 2:1–12)

The chief priests and the elders questioning Jesus' authority (Matthew 21:23–27)

Who Paul Had Become

Paul begins by describing how changed he is (Galatians 1:13–14, 22–24). His radical conversion gave credence to his message that his opponents could not claim.

- *Paul's previous life before Christ was famous or, rather, infamous. What was well-known about his treatment of Christians in those days (v. 13)?*

- *What was Paul's motivation to treat those early Christians so badly (v. 14)? How did he compare in his devotion to other Jews?*

His personal history was well-known inside and outside Jewish circles. For the Jewish leaders who were hostile to the Christian faith, Paul was something of a hero. Devout, consistent, and radical, he was willing to go to any length to put an end to this new "cult."

To Christians, however, Paul was a notorious terrorist. The early Christians had met in temple courts, but it was no longer safe there. They also met in homes, but Paul went from house to house to find them (Acts 8:1–3). They fled to other cities hundreds of kilometers away, but he even got letters from the authorities to pursue them there (9:1–2). Nowhere was a Christian safe from Paul.

"But then God called me by his grace" (Galatians 1:15), Paul declared, and he would never be the same. He still remained zealous but in the opposite direction. Imagine the captain of your favorite college football team running the ball into his own goal over and over again. No wonder both sides were confused over Paul! As J. P. Moreland states: "It's not the simple fact that Paul changed his views. You have to explain how he had this particular change of belief that completely went against his upbringing."[4]

What could account for this extreme change of heart? An encounter with Christians? Not a chance! Paul had met hundreds of them. He even heard the mighty Stephen preach, and that had no impact on him. He just went on grinding Christians under his feet.

Could social pressure have changed him? Again, as Paul wrote in Galatians 1:10, this would have led him to opposite conclusions. He already had the praise of his peers and mentors. Converting would gain him no friends there. Even the Christians were unwelcoming to him after his change of heart. There was simply no social incentive to switch sides.

Then what did make the change? Moreland explains: "He tells us himself what caused him to take a 180-degree turn and become the chief proponent of the Christian faith. By his own pen he says he saw the risen Christ and heard Christ appoint him to be one of his followers."[5]

- *A testimony of personal conversion is a powerful apologetic (defense) for the Christian faith. It can be disregarded by your audience, but it cannot be denied. Paul describes conversion in 2 Corinthians 5:17 as a transformation, a new creation. How has your life demonstrably changed since following Jesus? How could you be described as a new creation? What old things are gone, and what new things have come?*

- *Paul's conversion was so dramatic and so complete that eventually believers changed their tune about him. Did Paul have to preach or minister among them for this to happen (Galatians 1:21–24)? What was the response of Christians then?*

Who Sent Paul Out

Paul makes a second claim that his opponents could not use to bolster their message. Paul tells us that the way God called him by his grace was to reveal his Son directly and not through interaction with others (Galatians 1:16). In dramatic fashion, like unveiling a painting, the curtain was pulled back, and Paul got a supernatural vision of the glorious, resurrected Jesus.

- *From his first moments as a follower of Jesus, Paul knew his target audience. To whom would his mission efforts be directed (vv. 15–16)?*

- *According to Paul, when did God set him apart for his ground-breaking apostolic work? Since he hadn't responded to the grace of the Lord in previous decades, what could this mean?*

- *Did Paul seek out any human leaders for advice right after his encounter with Jesus (vv. 16–17)? What did he actually do?*

 DIGGING DEEPER

What was in Arabia? Desert. Wilderness. Solitude. And gentiles. Many scholars see in this Arabian journey a parallel to God's revelation of the law to Moses. Indeed, when Arabia is mentioned next (Galatians 4:25), it is a reference to Sinai and the old covenant. Scholars suggest this journey was a spiritual retreat of sorts where Paul learned the gospel of the new covenant from the Lord Jesus.

Others see in his Arabian journey the first steps of his mission to gentiles. Because he was already preaching immediately after his baptism (Acts 9:20–22), they argue the gospel had already been revealed to him, probably during the three days of blindness while he was fasting and praying (vv. 9, 11).

Whatever happened in Arabia, Paul's point in this detail is that he went away from other Christian influence rather than toward it. It would have been natural and expected at that point for Paul to go to Jerusalem, the birthplace and epicenter of the Christian movement. He could have joined in the vibrant life of the first church there. He could have sat under the teaching of the apostles. He could have been a disciple of the Twelve. But he did not need their input in that way because he had been taught the good news by Jesus himself. So instead of heading toward the church in Jerusalem, he went off by himself with the Lord, first to Arabia and then back to Damascus.

- *Unlike Paul, we learned about Jesus from other Christians. From whom did you learn about the good news? Where were you? Why were you sure this person or persons were trustworthy?*

Who Welcomed Paul

The final point Paul makes that his opponents cannot is the welcome he received from the Christian community and its key leaders.

- *How much time went by before Paul sought out his contemporary Christian leaders (Galatians 1:18–19)? Where did he meet with them? Why did he go to them? Whom did he see first?*

- *What other leader did he meet on that journey? What title does Paul give him to distinguish him?*

- *Paul feels compelled to insist on the truthfulness of this claim (v. 20). He anticipates that some of his readers will doubt him. Why do you think some of his readers might have distrusted him?*

THE BACKSTORY

Peter, of course, was the chief among the apostles. He was their leader and the one Jesus called out for special recognition (Matthew 16:18). From his first mention in the Gospels, his impetuous responses to Jesus' teaching and ministry give us many insights about following Christ. His powerful preaching on the day of Pentecost (Acts 2) introduced thousands in Jerusalem to life in the Lord. His fearless ministry in the face of fierce opposition pointed still more people to Jesus and set an example for them in suffering (Acts 3–5). His endorsement of sharing the gospel with Samaritans (8:14–17) and God-fearing gentiles (10:44–48) opened the door to new people groups.

This Jacob (also translated *James* in other Bible versions) that Paul mentions in Galatians was the Lord's half-brother and the non-apostle leader of the Christians in Jerusalem. While he was not a follower of Jesus before the resurrection, Jesus made a special appearance to him afterward (1 Corinthians 15:7), and Jacob became a faithful disciple from then on. Later, his mature and godly leadership would help to resolve definitively the same issue that was destroying the Galatians' faith (Acts 15).

John called himself "the disciple whom Jesus loved" (John 13:23; 19:26; 20:2; 21:7, 20), so some have described John as Jesus' closest friend. John was a partner in Peter's fishing business when Jesus called them both to follow him (Luke 5:7–10). Along with John's brother Jacob, the three made up Jesus' inner circle. They were there the first time Jesus raised the dead (Mark 5:37–42), when Jesus was transfigured on the mountain (9:1–8), and as close as possible when Jesus prayed in Gethsemane before his trial (14:32–36). With Peter, John was sent to verify that the first Samaritan converts were legitimate Christ-followers.

Peter and Jacob were pillars of the early church in Jerusalem, so it was fitting that Paul should meet with them, if only for a short visit. It would be fourteen years before Paul returned.

Paul in Jerusalem

• *When Paul returned to Jerusalem, did he go alone (Galatians 2:1)? Who was with him?*

- *What motivated him to go (2:2)? What was the agenda when he arrived this time? What did Paul explain to these leaders in Jerusalem? Why do you think the meeting was held privately?*

- *How long had Paul been preaching the good news by this point (v. 1)? In what ways could his work among gentiles have been in vain? What does this worry have to do with Titus (vv. 3–4)?*

- *What was the strategic value of bringing along Barnabas, a Jewish believer who was well-respected in Jerusalem?*

- *What was the strategic value of bringing along Titus, a convert through Paul's preaching and an uncircumcised gentile?*

- *What controversy led to this conference (vv. 4–5)? Who instigated the issue? How does Paul describe their motives?*

- *What posture did Paul take toward the infiltrators? What was the result of his steadfastness to the gospel (v. 5)?*

The reception of gentile believers into the Christian movement was controversial, so the apostles needed to address this simmering issue. How would the other leaders regard Paul's message? How would they assess his ministry? How would they treat his gentile colleague?

- *Remembering that Paul learned the gospel from Jesus in an unconventional way, what did the apostles and church leaders conclude about his message (vv. 6–10)?*

- *What did they recognize about Paul's specific ministry calling? How did his ministry compare to Peter's (vv. 7–9)?*

- *Was the presence of Titus an impediment to Christian fellowship and unity? What did all the leaders determine about how Paul and Barnabas should deal with gentiles like Titus (vv. 1–3, 9)?*

Paul's meeting with these senior leaders was a complete triumph! His message, his mission, and his associates had the stamp of approval. He could continue to confidently declare the good news with the full authority of Christ and the whole Christian church. This conference should have put the whole controversy to bed, but the letter to the Galatians proves there was more convincing to do.

Paul's recounting of his story detailed for the Galatians his unique qualifications to define and teach the good news. Because he was transformed by it, because Jesus revealed it to him directly, and because key church leaders endorsed his gospel-centered ministry, they could trust him. He was a credible witness, and they had to take him seriously.

EXPERIENCE GOD'S HEART

- *Even though we learned the good news from other Christians, it is still important for us to have personal encounters with God. Can you recall a time when you knew that God was speaking to you? Describe it. How do you know it was God? What was the message he was trying to get across?*

- *When we do not have a direct revelation like Paul, we can still be confident that we can hear from God through his Word, the Bible. Maybe that is why you are participating in this study. What are your Bible reading habits like? How often, where, and when do you read? Do meditation and prayer have a role in your Bible intake? If so, in what ways?*

♥ SHARE GOD'S HEART

- *Paul met with Peter, James, and others to explain the message he had been preaching to the gentiles. Likewise, it is good for us to articulate the gospel to a friendly audience. With a group of other believers, share the good news with each other. Tell one another the stories of how you came to faith in Jesus. Explain why someone should follow Jesus. The experience will improve your ability to communicate this life-giving message to non-believers.*

- *Once you have practiced articulating the good news, think of someone you know who has never heard about your spiritual journey. Pray for an opportunity to share it with him or her soon.*

Talking It Out

1. After years of teaching the gospel, Paul presented his message to the apostles, and they saw no need to improve on it. Discuss with others how our understanding of the good news can deepen or be clarified over time. How has your own appreciation or comprehension of the gospel improved with your growth toward spiritual maturity? How have you changed the way you talk about Jesus with others as you have grown in your faith?

2. Since we do not usually learn the gospel by independent divine revelation, what are some steps believers can take to get well-grounded in their understanding and communication of the good news? Should they go to seminary? What is the role of a local Bible class? Church services? Television or radio ministry? Podcasts? After writing down some steps you think are worthwhile, discuss with others to learn what they do to become better equipped to grasp and articulate the gospel of Jesus Christ.

LESSON 3

Peter, Paul, and the Rest of Us

(Galatians 2:11–21)

"You are the man!" declared the prophet, his icy glare freezing the king's heart with dread, his pointed finger penetrating to his soul.

Caught.

Exposed.

Obviously guilty and with nowhere to hide.

When the prophet Nathan confronted King David about his adultery with Bathsheba and his conspiracy against Uriah, David was undone (2 Samuel 12:1–13).

Then David did something extraordinary, something vanishingly rare among leaders. He admitted his sin. This important, admired ruler humbled himself and confessed. He did not try to justify himself. He did not deny what he had done. Instead, he confessed his sin. This response of contrite repentance resulted in mercy from God.

Confrontation led to humiliation. Humiliation led to humble repentance. And humble repentance led to forgiveness and freedom (Psalm 32:1–5). Sometimes, confrontation is exactly what is called for. Without it, people carry on as before, unchallenged and unchanged. Confrontation cuts through the pretense and presents the confronted with an opportunity to turn and recalibrate.

A Quarrel at the Supper Table

Before Paul launched into the main argument of his letter to the Galatians, he had one more bit of backstory to tell. Again, he meant for this element to add to his credibility on the principal problem of Galatians. This time, Paul described an encounter with Peter, a family quarrel at the supper table. A confrontation with the chief apostle over the nature of the good news.

- *Who was this Peter that Paul mentions (Galatians 2:11; see also John 1:42)?*

- *How did Peter treat the gentile believers when he first arrived in Antioch (Galatians 2:12)?*

- *Looking over the context (vv. 11–16), how did Paul describe the men who arrived from Jerusalem? How did Peter change his behavior toward the gentiles after they arrived? Why did he do this?*

- *What effect did Peter's change of behavior have on the other Jewish Christians (v. 13)?*

 THE BACKSTORY

It is difficult for modern Westerners, with our microwave-able frozen food and bagged lunches, to understand the ancient Middle Eastern significance of breaking bread together. The care and attention given to providing and preparing life-sustaining food for guests had symbolic as well as practical value. Generous hospitality was a highly esteemed and culturally powerful expression of friendship.

We see this in the parable Jesus told of the friend coming to the door at midnight asking for bread (Luke 11:5–8). When a guest arrived at the house, no matter what the hour, the host was obliged to share his food. Having nothing in the house for his own family to eat was acceptable. Having nothing to share with a guest was an absolute no-no. It would be better to pester another friend out of bed, rousing his whole family from their slumber, to make sure there was bread to share with the guest. Jesus assumes that everyone hearing his parable would feel that way about the hospitality of sharing food.

Furthermore, a shared meal was tangible communion with one another. It was a profound symbol of acceptance, perhaps agreement, and identification. Withholding table fellowship from the disreputable was expected of a holy Jew. That's why the Pharisees were shocked that Jesus sat at the table with known "sinners" like tax-collectors, prostitutes, gluttons, and drunks (see, for example, Matthew 11:19; Mark 2:15–17; 7:2–5; Luke 15:1–2).

While eating specific unclean food was forbidden to Jews, eating with gentiles was never prohibited in the law of Moses. However, after the Jews returned from exile to Palestine, a new, more strident version of Judaism took hold. Through the efforts of scribes and Pharisees, extra rules grew up around the law. These rules were meant to keep the faithful at a safe distance from sin. If explicit sin was the edge of a cliff, Pharisaic Judaism moved the moral boundaries a hundred feet back from the dangerous edge.

Since gentiles had few scruples about foods, it was likely that some off-limits ingredients would be consumed at their tables

(Daniel 1:5, 8). To keep the food laws, it was safest not to eat with gentiles at all. What was safest became expected and eventually demanded. So for the observant first-century Jew, eating with gentiles was simply scandalous.

Some teachers see in Galatians 2 the sharing of a Eucharistic meal. Doubtless, the participants were remembering the Lord while they ate (even though the formalities of the liturgy were still unimaginable at this early stage of the church), but it isn't necessary for us to see communion around a formal Christian ritual as the chief problem here. Jews, even Christian Jews, at any table with gentiles was the dilemma.

Peter had already been scolded by some for eating with gentiles of Cornelius' household (Acts 11:1–3) and had defended himself confidently (vv. 17–18). However, that single defense was clearly not enough to halt the swirling controversy. Its continuing impact was evident in Antioch.

- *What sin did Paul accuse Peter of (Galatians 2:13)? Does Paul's judgment seem harsh for the situation or not harsh enough?*

- *Why did Paul come to his conclusion (v. 14)? How were Peter's actions out of sync with the gospel message?*

🔶 WORD WEALTH

The word *hypocrite* gets tossed around a lot, usually to discredit someone for acting inconsistently with their values. For example, when a smoker tells someone they should not smoke, it is sometimes referred to as hypocrisy. Or urging others to read Scripture every day while failing to do it ourselves. To be precise, this isn't really hypocrisy. It is simply falling short of one's own ideals. Often, it is exhorting others to aim higher than our own achievements.

Hypocrisy is a direct English alliteration of the Greek word *hupokrisis*. In extra-biblical literature, the word described an actor on the stage playing a role, pretending to be someone else. It meant expressing the words and attitudes of someone else. It meant putting on the costume, the mask, and the persona of someone they were not. It meant impersonation.

Hypocrisy in the Bible is wearing a mask. It is play-acting that we are the sort of person that we are not. It is pretending to achieve a moral standard when we have not. Often it is pretending to be more righteous than we are. It is looking righteous on the surface while harboring wickedness in the heart, as when Jesus accused the Pharisees of it (see Matthew 23:27–28; Luke 12:1). However, hypocrisy can also be pretending to have convictions we don't truly have in order to impress others. That was Peter's hypocrisy in this instance.

- *What conviction was Peter pretending to have? Why do you think the others (even Barnabas!) were swept up in it?*

- *What would gentile believers have concluded from Peter's actions toward them? What false impressions of the gospel was Peter communicating?*

- *Paul couldn't take this hypocrisy sitting down. How did he respond to Peter's behavior (Galatians 2:11, 14)?*

Peter Publicly Rebuked

The fierceness of Paul's confrontation is startling, especially when we recognize how similar Paul and Peter were in their backgrounds and religious convictions. Both Peter and Paul were cultural and observant Jews. They followed the food laws, the feasts, the obligations, and the moral code of Moses. Both were called in-person by Jesus to follow him: Peter on the shores of Lake Galilee (Luke 5:1–11) and Paul on the road to Damascus. Both were appointed as Jesus' apostles, Peter to the Jews and Paul to the gentiles.

Despite their specific assignments, both were also instrumental in reaching gentiles with Jesus' good news. They both enthusiastically endorsed and celebrated gentiles embracing the Jewish Messiah. Paul thought they should agree about this too.

- *Paul pointed out that their common experience as Jews prepared them for the truth of the gospel. What do Jews know about the law that gentiles do not know (Galatians 2:15–16)?*

- *What must Jews do to be justified (made righteous) before God (v. 16)? What can the law never do for any of us?*

- *Does our "desire to be righteous through our union with the Anointed One…mean [that] our Messiah condones sin" (v. 17)? Why or why not?*

- *Read verse 18. Paul's point here is that if we return to the "old religious system"—life under the Mosaic law—after embracing the gospel of grace that justifies us apart from the law, the law would yet again show us to be lawbreakers, sinners. Based on what Paul has said about the law so far in his letter, what reason(s) do you think he would cite for making such a statement? In other words, what would have to be true about the law to make Paul's statement here accurate?*

- *Now consider what Peter had done before Paul arrived in Antioch. At first Peter "enjoyed eating with the gentile believers who didn't keep the Jewish customs" (v. 12). But when Jacob's Jewish friends arrived, Peter refused to eat with those same gentile believers (vv. 12–13). Were Peter's actions an example of embracing the gospel of grace and then returning to the law, to the old religious system? Explain your answer.*

Some Jewish believers objected to the new gospel reality. For them to practice the good news of Jesus consistently, they would be sharing life with un-Judaized gentiles. This was such a cultural taboo for Jews reared in Pharisaic Judaism that it seemed like sin. The implication, then, was that embracing the gospel was embracing sin.

Paul swatted this objection aside. It was not sinful to implement the gospel in this way; it was sinful not to. Restoring old divisions based on ethnic rituals and keeping the law was not righteousness. If those old walls needed rebuilding, then it was sin to knock them down in the first place! Demanding that gentile believers keep the law to have full fellowship with Jewish believers taught all the wrong ideas about the gospel.

In this passage, Paul made the first reference to the contrast between faith and works, a major theme of Galatians: Are sinners made righteous before God through good faith or good works? We will explore more about this when we come to Galatians 3.

🄷 WORD WEALTH

We often use the word *justify* to mean defending a wrong action or attitude. We justify our behavior. We justify our feelings. We were justified in our response to this or that action. By our reason, we explain how wrong is right. This use of the word has only a sliver of connection to the biblical idea of justification.

In the Bible, especially in Romans and Galatians, a person in the wrong is justified when God makes them right. It is a legal term for when a defendant stands before the judge and the judge declares him innocent. A judge can do this for the truly innocent, but he can also do this for the guilty. In either case, the judge can declare the defendant innocent, just as if he had never sinned.

Our sin makes us all guilty before God. We have no excuses. No good deed can erase our sin. On our own, we are stuck with our wrongs, and we cannot be righted. So God mercifully steps in. Through the righteous life of Jesus and his willing death for our sins, our debt is paid, our sin is covered, and we are justified through faith in him.

Biblical justification happens when God judges a sinner to be righteous. Justification is "the favourable verdict of God, the

Righteous Judge, that one who formerly stood condemned has now been granted a new status at the bar of divine justice."[6] Justification does not come from our own ability to *do* what is right. It comes from *faith* in Jesus, who accomplished righteousness for us.

Living the New Life

The Christian life is described succinctly in Galatians 2:19–20 as total identification with Christ. This is a bit mystical sounding at first, but here's how it works:

By faith, we are included in the eternal life of Jesus. We identify with him in his death and his resurrection. When Jesus died, we died. When he rose from the dead, we rose from the dead. Just as he goes on living the new life forever, we live the new life. All in him. All with him. All through him.

- *With this in mind, what step must a person take to live for God (vv. 19–20)?*

- *How is a Christian able to live the righteous life? What is the means of joining into this new life (v. 20)?*

- *In what two ways does Paul explain that Jesus identified with us (v. 20)? Can you think of some other possible ways that he doesn't list (e.g., physical birth, human parents, and ethnicity)?*

- *If we could be righteous or earn righteousness some other way, what was the point of Jesus' death (v. 21)?*

When Was Peter Confronted?

Paul's recollections in Galatians help to fill in the timeline of Paul's life and the early Christian movement found in Acts. Synthesizing the two accounts gives a fuller understanding of how the Galatians controversy developed.

- *Look up the passages in the empty timeline provided to fill in the key events leading up to the Council of Jerusalem, where this issue was addressed. (The answer key for this timeline is in the Appendix at the end of this study guide.)*

Acts	Galatains	Event/era leading to Jerusalem council	30	35	40	45	50
		Jesus' death, resurrection, and ascension	●				
8:1–3; 9:1–2	1:13–14		▬				
9:3–19a	1:15–16a		●				
	1:16b–17		●				
9:19b–22	1:17		▬				
9:26–29	1:18–20			●			
	1:21						
10:1–11:18				▬▬▬	▬▬▬		
11:19–24							
	1:22–2:10					●	
11:25–26						▬	
11:27–30						●	
13:1–14:25						●	
14:26–28							
	2:11–16					●	
		Galations Written				●	
15:1–6							●

When Paul and Barnabas returned from their mission through Galatia, they went back to Antioch to give a report and to teach among the Christian community there. It was during this lengthy span of local ministry that Peter came to visit.

 DIGGING DEEPER

It has been said, "You must learn from the mistakes of others. You will never live long enough to make them all yourself." Apart from Pharaoh, no biblical character was rebuked more than the apostle Peter. In every case (besides this one in Galatians), it was the Lord Jesus himself doing the confronting.

• *Look up the passages and fill in the grid. What do we learn from Peter's mistakes?*

Rebuke	Occasion	What error was confronted?	What can we learn from Peter's mistake?
Matthew 14:25–33			
Matthew 16:21–23			
Matthew 26:50–54			

Mark 14:27–31			
Mark 14:32–38			
Luke 5:1–11			
Luke 22:54–62			
John 13:3–11			
John 21:15–22			
Acts 10:9–16			
Galatians 2:11–16			

We shouldn't be too critical of faithful Peter. He was bold and impetuous, to be sure. That led him to make great boasts and take great risks. We can learn more from the times Peter got it wrong, recognizing that the track record of the other apostles was not great either.

Good Results

What were the results of the Peter-and-Paul confrontation in Galatians 2:11? We don't know how this awkward conversation ended. From the text, we don't even know when Paul's words to Peter morph into Paul's words to the Galatians (the original Greek text has no quotation marks). But the rebuke appears to have had a positive and lasting impact on Peter, Paul, and the rest of us.

Months later in Jerusalem (Acts 15:1–29), Peter and Paul stood on the same side of the controversy over Judaizing gentiles. At that meeting, Peter made the case that Paul made to him in Antioch. The unity that grew out of their conflict stabilized the fledgling multi-ethnic Christian movement. Their ultimate cooperation on this treacherous controversy prevented the church from splintering and continues to enable worldwide Christian cross-cultural missions today.

EXPERIENCE GOD'S HEART

It is still tempting for us to show Peter's kind of hypocrisy, isn't it? A person or group we admire holds to a particular lifestyle or doctrinal conviction, so we try to conform to please them even when we don't fully agree with them. Most of the time, it is about a minor issue and can be overlooked, but sometimes, like over the meals in Antioch, the issue is more central than that.

- *Have you ever pretended to believe something to impress others or to remain in favor with them? Describe the situation.*

- *Have you ever been pressured to do something, even something good, that you didn't believe in? What happened?*

- *Paul had a harsh word for Peter. He could have deferred to him as the elder apostle. He could have stifled his irritation and let the matter alone. But he didn't. Have you ever had to confront someone, perhaps harshly? If so, what drove you to risk that confrontation? How was it received? What was the ultimate outcome?*

- *Peter received a harsh word from Paul. From all the evidence, it seems that he took it well. The results, at least, were good for him and the church. Have you ever been confronted by a friend? How would you describe their tone? In hindsight, how do you feel about that moment? How did you first respond to it? Did you defend yourself, or did you humble yourself?*

 SHARE GOD'S HEART

- *Every believer in Jesus lives the new life by faith in the Son of God who loved us and gave himself for us (Galatians 2:20). What does it mean to you that God loves you personally and gave himself for you personally?*

• *How have you responded to that kind of love?*

• *Is this the kind of message you can keep to yourself? Why or why not?*

• *What difference could it make to others that God loves them enough to send his Son for them? How might it change their view of God? How might it change their view of themselves?*

Talking It Out

1. How different things might have been if Paul had not dared to confront Peter or if Peter had responded in anger or defensiveness. Discuss how unaccountable leadership can bring trouble. Under what circumstances would you be willing to confront a leader?

2. What kind of group dynamics promote the hypocrisy of pretending to have convictions you don't really have? Discuss some examples from your experience and what steps a small group could take to avoid them.

LESSON 4

How to Arrive at Righteousness

(Galatians 3:1–14)

A missionary travels regularly into the Himalayas to minister in a village so remote that no road goes there and on the side of a mountain so rugged that no airstrip can be built there. For more than ten years, he has been revisiting this group that the rest of the world barely knows about, but the first time he could never have found it on his own. He needed to follow a skilled guide who had been there before, someone familiar with the path. The journey there is hard, all on foot along treacherous gravel paths. The trek takes several days. These visits take extraordinary commitment on the missionary's part.

Why walk that far? Simply put, there is no other way. Jeep travel might at first seem a better and faster means to make such a long journey, but there are no roads. Trying to get there by car would be ridiculous and foolish. Planes can go to great altitudes, but if they cannot land, they are little help. To insist on taking a plane where a plane cannot go is beyond foolish!

Paul began Galatians with a lengthy rehearsal of his biographical credentials, including a confrontation with Peter over the practical implications of the gospel. Now he turns to the whole reason for his letter: a confrontation with the Galatian believers about the nature of the gospel. The good news is about what it takes to be made right with God. It answers the question, *What is God's way to get to righteousness?*

Remember, Galatians is an urgent letter. The tone of the next section makes this clear. It was written to address an immediate theological danger. It was written to correct a growing threat to these young churches, one that Paul had hoped they would be immune to. The apostle writes harshly in hopes that his correction is not too late.

- *How can we tell that Paul is frustrated with these churches he established in Galatia (Galatians 3:1, 3, 4)? What words does he use to describe the Galatians? What phrases indicate that the problem is both spiritual and rational? What is irrational about the Galatians' embracing this false gospel?*

- *What fact about Jesus is central to the gospel (v. 1)?*

• *In two rhetorical questions, Paul mentions signs of God's genuine work among the Galatians. What are they (vv. 2, 5)? What is the obvious answer to these rhetorical questions?*

• *Paul contrasts faith with works. Do you see another contrast in this passage (v. 3)?*

Paul begins by calling his readers foolish. Other translations use silly, thoughtless, irrational, stupid, senseless, crazy, idiotic, and unwitting. No compliments there! You may catch more flies with honey than vinegar, but you get more attention with a slap than a hug.

It seems at first that Paul is insulting his readers' intelligence, that they don't have the wits to understand what is happening to them. But there is also a moral and spiritual component to his accusation. They have been bewitched or spiritually hexed. Brian Simmons explains, "The Greek word used here means 'to cast a spell using the evil eye.' Paul uses a pun here in the Greek text. He goes on to say, 'Didn't God *open* your eyes?'"[7]

The Christians of Galatia had suffered for their simple faith in the crucified Jesus (3:4). Now they were turning away toward a different, more complex message, one that made their works the key to all God has already provided for them. That's foolish!

🌀 DIGGING DEEPER

Throughout Galatians, we are urged to choose the living way of faith rather than the dead-end road of works. Works of righteousness are, of course, commendable and expected of God's people. Wouldn't it be a tragedy if believers did no good works at all? That would be confusing, to say the least. Paul never encouraged his readers to abandon good works or to perform evil ones.

The problem with our good works, Paul explains, is when we believe that they *justify* us before God. If we believe that we can do enough good to meet God's standard, if we believe that our behavior is the measure of God's approval, if we believe that we can somehow do all the right and necessary things to achieve salvation, we are doomed. That road will never get us to righteousness (Galatians 2:15–16).

Good works are a dead end for three reasons. First, God's standard is higher than ours (Isaiah 64:6), and, let's be honest, we have never even measured up to our own standards (Romans 2:14–15). Second, good deeds cannot undo evil deeds we've done. So even if we do more good than bad, we haven't cleaned the slate. We need a cleansing that only God can provide (Psalm 51:7–9). Third, God has provided a works-free way of righteousness at immeasurable personal cost (Romans 3:21–24; 2 Corinthians 5:21). To turn our noses up at that offer while striving to achieve it by good works shows contempt for the Lord (Galatians 2:21).

The truly saving alternative to works is faith. Faith means believing what God has said and trusting in what Jesus has done (Galatians 2:19–20). It is realizing that our own works will always fall short and leave us stranded short of real righteousness (Romans

3:10, 23). It is trusting that we can do nothing, but Jesus has done everything. He lived perfect righteousness (Hebrews 4:15), he died the death we deserved (Romans 5:6–8), and he rose again to give life to anyone who will believe in him (John 11:24–25).

Good works, then, cannot produce righteousness. Instead, they are the product of the righteousness we receive by faith. We will see this clearly when we explore Galatians 5.

Abraham Got There First

- *Whom does Paul introduce as the first guide to righteousness (Galatians 3:6)? How did this person arrive at righteousness?*

- *What makes us the spiritual children of Abraham (vv. 7, 9)?*

- *Why should the salvation of the gentiles have been anticipated by the Jews (vv. 8–9)? What was God's plan to make gentiles righteous? Is it any different than his plan for Jews?*

- *Were there any cultural or geographical limitations to God's promise to Abraham? How is that good news?*

- *What admirable title does Paul give to Abraham (v. 6)?*

 THE BACKSTORY

Abraham is important as a model of faith because Jewish believers thought of him as their spiritual father, the founder of their religion. They hearkened back to him for their cultural and spiritual identity. And, importantly for gentile believers, Abraham was not a Jew. He preceded Moses and the law. He even preceded covenantal circumcision. He arrived at righteousness with God before any aspect of cultural Judaism existed. So he can be a guide to righteousness for both Jews and gentiles.

To make his case, Paul quotes two promises of God given to Abraham. The first is taken from Genesis 15:1–6. On a cloudless night in Canaan, the old man Abraham wondered aloud to God about his promises. The Lord directed Abraham's eyes to the sky and told him that his descendants would be as numerous as the stars. To a centenarian with a wife already decades beyond menopause and no children between them, this was an outlandish promise for Abraham to believe. But he did believe. He simply trusted what God said. This faith made him righteous.

Abraham offered no sacrifice. He received no law. He performed no religious rites. He completed no outward acts of righteousness. Abraham just put his faith in God's word to him.

The other Scripture quoted comes from Abraham's first encounter with the Lord (see Genesis 12:1–4). Again, not based on anything that Abraham did, God made promises to Abraham (at that time called Abram). Extravagant promises of blessing for himself, blessing for those who blessed him, and blessing for all the nations. No works could earn this kind of generosity from God. Abraham only had to believe.

Faith was the way Abraham got to righteousness. And it was still the way that Jews and gentiles of Paul's day got to righteousness. Faith has always been and still is the only way.

ⓒ DIGGING DEEPER

From today's perspective, there is little doubt that Christianity is a gentile movement. Ethnic Jews make up a fraction of a fraction of a percent of those who have received by faith the good news of Jesus. However, in the first decades of Christianity, the church was predominantly a sect of Judaism.

God's covenant with Abraham was never nation specific. God's blessings were always meant to be international and multicultural. Because of Father Abraham, Jews should have seen gentile salvation coming.

Jews had come to see their place with God as an exclusive privilege to be protected. This is obvious from Paul and Barnabas' first mission forays into Galatia as the message began to take hold among ordinary gentiles. They began there by proclaiming the good news in the synagogue to Jews and gentile converts to Judaism. As the response to their message grew in the rest of the city, Jewish opponents drove them away.

Paul responded by reminding them of God's heart for the whole world:

> We were compelled to bring God's
> message first to you Jews. But seeing
> you've rejected this message and refuse to
> embrace eternal life, we will focus instead
> on the nations [gentiles] and offer it to
> them. This will fulfill what the Lord has
> commanded us: "I have destined you to
> become a beacon light for the nations and
> release salvation to the ends of the earth!"
> (Acts 13:46–47)

Paul quotes from the prophet Isaiah (49:6), which is only one of hundreds of Scripture passages that indicate God's salvation was always meant for the whole world. The New Testament mission to "go into all the world [and] preach openly the wonderful news of the gospel" (Mark 16:15) is not a change in God's plan. It is the fuller, deeper expression of what God meant to happen all along.[8]

- *Look up each passage below and jot down next to each what you learn about God and his plan for all the world.*

    Genesis 12:1–3

    Psalm 22:27–28

    Psalm 67

    Psalm 96:1–10

    Isaiah 2:1–4

    Isaiah 49:3–7

    Micah 4:1–4

The Religious Road to Nowhere

Paul then turns from the one reliable way for getting to righteousness to one reliable way *not* to. The way not to puts us under a curse, and that is the way of human works. Anyone who hopes in his or her own good works to get to righteousness will never arrive.

- *Whom does Paul say are under a curse (Galatians 3:10–12)? What is the level of obedience demanded if we are going to go the law-keeping route? Who is capable of meeting this standard?*

- *Why is righteousness by faith contrary to the law (v. 12)? What is the law based on?*

Working our way to righteousness is impossible. To drop the ball in any area is to fall short of the standard (Romans 3:23). If we choose this route, we must go all the way, but none of us can. Only one person has ever lived up to God's standard—Jesus Christ (2 Corinthians 5:21; Hebrews 4:14–15).

But we do try. Every religious system, apart from the good news, depends on good works. Judaism has the law of Moses. Buddhism has the Eight-Fold Path. Islam has its Five Pillars. Even some forms of Christianity place heavy emphasis on works you must perform to get in and stay in God's grace. And when we don't have a formal religious system, we still have an unwritten moral code we feel we must adhere to if we're going to be righteous.

An English traveler was hopelessly lost and in need of directions in the rugged west of Ireland. Eventually, he came upon a farmer cutting peat in a remote bog. The tourist stepped out of his car and slowly made his way across the soft ground, calling out, "Can you tell me how I would get to Letterfrack?"

The farmer began to explain in a round-about fashion the round-about way of getting to the man's desired destination. The directions were colorful but complicated, providing more confusion than clarity. The English guest asked more and more questions in growing frustration. The Irish farmer offered more and more answers, patiently and unsuccessfully. Finally, the traveler threw his hands up in despair and walked back toward his car.

As he walked away, his unperturbed guide called out one more word of advice: "To be honest, friend, if I were going to Letterfrack, I wouldn't start from here."[9]

We all start out as people striving to do good works. Paul says that means we all start out cursed. To begin cursed and falling short of righteousness is a bad place to start. If you want to get to righteousness, you wouldn't want to start from here. You just can't get there from here, at least not apart from divine provision.

Paul's message to the Galatians is that no works can get us to righteousness. Only Jesus can get us there.

The Only Guide to Where We Are Going

• *Since we all start out cursed, what is the way out of it (Galatians 3:13)? Who took our curse for us?*

- *Could anyone else have done what Christ did (2 Corinthians 5:21)? Why or why not?*

- *How did God include gentiles in the blessings of Abraham (Galatians 3:13–14)?*

- *How can anyone, even gentiles, access these riches (v. 14)?*

- *What is the evidence that gentiles belong to God's covenant people (vv. 2, 14)?*

Jesus took the curse for us. No one else could. He could because he had achieved the righteousness that eludes the rest of us. He wasn't cursed because he was hanged on a tree; he was hanged on a tree because he was cursed. A merciless conspiracy of Jews and gentiles condemned or cursed him to die on the cross.

Jesus freely took on our curse so that all the nations, Jew and gentile, could receive the blessings of Abraham. He did this so that the gentiles could be included in the covenant people of God. He did this so that we could all get to righteousness through him. Our works couldn't get us there, but faith can. By faith in him, we arrive at righteousness.

🅐 WORD WEALTH

"Redeemed, how I love to proclaim it. Redeemed by the blood of the Lamb" goes the old hymn.[10] When we understand redemption, how can we help but sing?

Redemption was a common concept in the law of Moses. The law commanded that every firstborn be redeemed (Exodus 13:11–16). After God rescued all firstborn of Israel from the angel of death, every firstborn man or beast belonged to God. So a faithful Israelite could give the animal back to God through sacrifice or make a sacrifice in place of the firstborn. Either way, the price for a life was a life.

The word Paul used here, *exagorazo,* which is translated "redeemed" or "paid the full price" (Galatians 3:13), is built around the word *agora,* the marketplace where goods, products, and even slaves were bought and sold. Redemption means to pay off a ransom or to set someone free by paying a price. Redemption occurs when a new master buys a slave on the auction block only to set the slave free.

Redemption means we were up for sale as slaves. God saw us on the auction block and paid the price to free us. He didn't pay cash. The price for a life is a life. Not just any life would do to purchase all of us. It couldn't be the life of just another slave. It had to be the life of the only one who was truly free, Jesus. That's why Peter wrote, "You know that your lives were ransomed once and for all from the empty and futile way of life handed down from generation to generation. It was not a ransom payment of silver and gold, which eventually perishes, but the precious blood of Christ—who like a spotless, unblemished lamb was sacrificed for us" (1 Peter 1:18–19).

Do you want to know how valuable you are? Look at the cross where Jesus was crucified. See there the Righteous One dying for you, taking your curse, paying your ransom. That's how much you matter to God. That's how far he is willing to go to rescue and redeem you.

What a price! What a sacrifice! What love! "How I love to proclaim it!"

 # EXPERIENCE GOD'S HEART

- *Have you ever thought that you weren't enough for God?
  That your sins were too great or your goodness too small?
  Who told you that? Do you think that is a good or a bad
  starting point for responding to Jesus? Explain your answer.*

- *Jesus redeemed you by giving himself in your place. He paid your price and set you free. How does it make you feel to know that Jesus redeemed you? Are you grateful, humbled, sorry, thrilled? What emotions come to mind? Why?*

 SHARE GOD'S HEART

- *Abraham believed God. Paul says that believing God's promise is the secret to salvation. Does the faith of Abraham surprise you? What would you find difficult about believing the promise that he believed?*

- *What do people find difficult about believing the promise of Jesus' good news? Do you think their objections are mostly emotional or intellectual?*

- *Sometimes objections to the Christian message are intellectual. This barrier to faith calls for apologetics, the branch of theology that helps Christians defend or prove the truths of Scripture.[11] What experience do you have with Christian apologetics? When sharing your faith, have you ever used or needed apologetics?*

Talking It Out

1. Many religions and even some Christian groups teach that we can keep the rules and thereby secure whatever form of salvation they envision. Talk about why this is such a common human approach to reaching for God. Why do so many people think this approach will work?

2. Paul wrote this letter to groups of believers in Galatia. It was meant for the people to read and respond to as a religious community. As a group of believers, answer the questions Paul asked in Galatians 3:1–5, taking careful note of any of the questions that you struggle to answer.

LESSON 5

What the Law Did for Us

(Galatians 3:15–25)

From the beginning, Christians have had a complicated relationship with the law of Moses. Of course, we have the highest regard for the Hebrew Scriptures. New Testament faith grows out of Old Testament soil. At first, all the early church had was the Torah, the Psalms, and the Prophets. It took about forty years after Jesus' death and resurrection, or perhaps more, for the New Testament books to be composed and shared.[12] Until then, prophecies of the Messiah from Genesis through Malachi were what prepared the whole world for Jesus Christ.

Because the Old Testament is so important to Christians, some Christian groups advocate for keeping the law as best we can, excepting, of course, the sacrificial system described there. They believe the Mosaic law, as Scripture, should be obeyed and that the rules of the Old Testament are just as necessary as ever. These believers often worship and rest on Saturday (the Sabbath), follow the food and cleanliness laws, and celebrate the annual feasts prescribed in the Torah. They view the Christian faith as an extension of Judaism.[13]

However, this overlooks the simple fact that the new covenant *is* different from the old. The gospel of Jesus calls for a new understanding of Jewish teaching. The coming of the Messiah changes the way we see the writings that preceded him. The fulfillment of the law changes the way we view the law.

Many Christians take the opposite approach. In their view, now that Jesus has come and fulfilled the law, its usefulness is past. There's no need to learn the Old Testament or to study the law. The Old provides a helpful historical context but not much beyond that. These Christians often distribute copies of the New Testament because they believe these Scriptures are sufficient. The law of Moses is simply obsolete.

But this, too, is a distortion of the gospel truth. The law is quoted 126 times in the New Testament. Obviously, there remains a role for those Scriptures to the devoted follower of Jesus.

So while the law of Moses is no longer binding, it still has value. In Galatians 3:15–25, Paul sets out to explain this.

As we have learned, the Galatians were having difficulty in their own relationship with the law and rule keeping. They had been influenced by teachers who insisted that Jesus was necessary for salvation but not sufficient for salvation. According to these teachers, the rest of the steps that the gentiles needed were still found in keeping the law of Moses.

The apostle Paul adamantly and vehemently opposed that idea. To this point in the letter to the Galatians, Paul called this teaching a different gospel, a non-gospel, foolish, and fleshly. He called the promoters of this heresy confusers, false teachers, and cursed. He opposed their teaching viscerally, but as we will learn in this portion of the letter, he also opposed it historically.

To make his point, he went back into redemptive history. Before his contemporaries, before the apostles, before the kingdom of Israel, and the conquest of Canaan. He went back to a time before the law, before Moses, and even before the tribes of Israel. He went all the way back to the life of Abraham.

- *The Judaizers placed their confidence in the commands given to Moses in the law, but they also cherished their heritage in Abraham. How could a gentile believer of Paul's gospel teaching also reckon Abraham as their forefather (3:7–14)?*

Before the Law

High atop the mighty mountains of the western United States rest the glaciers that supply these arid states with water. Certainly, the occasional rain is a welcome godsend, but the reliable water that gives life to the land is in the annual runoff. This water is a precious resource, and many of the legal agreements about it are older than the states themselves.

As settlers laid claim to these vast lands, their homestead farms and ranches depended on a guaranteed source of water. The rights to this invaluable asset were secured through the legal doctrine of prior appropriation. Loosely, this means that the first to put the water to beneficial use has the right to its use.

Development that followed—railroads, mines, towns, dams, and roadways, even other settlers upstream—had to cooperate with these agreements. Even the sovereign states that formed out of these territories had to give deference to the water rights already in place. New laws would be added, but they were not allowed to supersede the older and still existing water rights.

How unpredictable and unreliable homesteading would have been if new governments or powerful individuals could cavalierly adopt new laws that laid waste to every agreement that came before! That's the point that Paul is about to make.

- *What everyday example does Paul use to put the law in perspective (v. 15)?*

- *The word Paul uses for covenant (or "contract," v. 15) can also mean a person's last will. When does a will go into effect? Once it has, who can change it? Can the heirs? Can the original testator?*

- *Whom did God include as recipients of the promises made to Abraham (Genesis 12:7; 13:15; 24:7)?*

- *According to Paul, are the Abrahamic recipients a specific people group or a specific person (Galatians 3:16)?*

- *Read Galatians 3:17–18. Which covenant was in place first, Abraham's or Moses'? How much older is this earlier covenant? Which, then, takes precedence?*

- *Did the law of Moses set aside the promise to Abraham? Does law-keeping replace promise-believing?*

- *What was the basis for the inheritance to Abraham (vv. 17–18)? Was it the law, or was it the promise?*

- *What motivated God to make the promise to Abraham (v. 18)? Was the promise made because of Abraham's character or behavior? Could the promise be unmade because of Abraham's character or behavior?*

Beneath the law of Moses rested the promise of Abraham. God's promise is older and better than the law. For one-quarter of Jewish history, there had been no law of Moses. Paul argued from this fact that the law is not the foundation of salvation, so it must not take precedence over the promise. The law is not the fundamental reality; it is an add-on.

Purpose of the Law

- *Think of an add-on to a building, a driver added on to your insurance policy, additional resources at the back of a book, add-ons to an internet browser, etc. What was the law added to and why (v. 19)? Who added the law?*

- *The law was given for a specific timeframe. What event closed out the era of the Mosaic law (v. 19)? How is the promise superior to the law in this regard?*

- *What is a messenger? Who were the messengers of the law (v. 19)?*

- *What is a mediator? Who was the mediator of the law? Was there a messenger or mediator of the promise (v. 20)?*

- *Did the law of God contradict, negate, or replace the foundational promises of God (v. 21)?*

- *What can faith in God's promises do that the law can never, never do (vv. 10–11, 17–18, 21)? Could the law give us the eternal life we need? Can it make us righteous?*

The law was added to the promise of Abraham. It was not added to negate it. Abraham's promise was not contradicted by the law. It was not added to supersede the promise. Moses did not replace Abraham. The law was not added to adjust or amend it. The law did not tweak God's older unconditional promise.

The promise predates the law. Unlike the law, it never expired. The promise came directly from God without intermediaries. Faith already provided the righteousness that the law could not.

 THE BACKSTORY

Paul mentions that angels first received the law, and then they passed it along to Moses. But when we turn back to the Exodus account of God giving the law, we don't find angels mentioned. Where did Paul get this idea about the role of angels, then? Bible scholar Timothy George explains:

> The Hebrew text of Exodus 19, which contains the scriptural account of the giving of the law, does not refer to angels, but it does describe Mount Sinai as surrounded by thunder, lightning, a thick cloud, and billows of fire (Exodus 19:16–19). Later Old Testament texts, notably the Septuagintal version of Deuteronomy 33:2 and Psalm 68:18, interpret these natural phenomena to mean that a large number of angels, the fiery hosts of heaven, accompanied God in his giving of the law at Sinai. The participation of the angels in the giving of the law was not merely a piece of pious Jewish folklore, for it is confirmed elsewhere in the New Testament (Acts 7:38, 53; Hebrews 2:2). Paul accepted this tradition and repeated it here [in Galatians 3:19].[14]

Addressing the Transgressing

If all that Paul has said up to this point in Galatians 3 is true, why was the law added at all? Paul anticipated this question. Surely, if God added the law, even for a little while, then the law is good. Furthermore, it must be good for something. But what?

- *Why was the law added (Galatians 3:19)? A transgression (or sin) is trespassing, crossing a line. How does the law address transgression? Why was that usefulness exhausted when the offspring of Abraham came?*

God gave the law because of transgressions "to show people their sins." There are two ways to understand this purpose. The law was given so that until the ultimate solution to our sin came, there would be a clear provision for sin. Much of the law of Moses presents a detailed description of temple worship: the priests, the offerings, the procedures for dealing with sin, and its consequence. In other words, until Jesus became the supreme atoning sacrifice, the temporary system of atonement was put in place.

Another purpose of the law is that it made clear what transgression is. The law revealed and exposed sin. As Paul wrote in Romans 7:7, "It was the law that gave us the clear definition of sin. For example, when the law said, 'Do not covet,' it became the catalyst to see how wrong it was for me to crave what belongs to someone else." We needed this clarity until the Seed of Abraham arrived. Until God's perfect righteousness was revealed in the Incarnate Son of God, we needed a clear understanding of sin and righteousness. The law did that for the world.

Jailing the Outlaws

The law revealed a righteousness that we could not attain. Before Jesus, no one ever kept the law. No one ever could. It set the standard, but the standard was too high. When we strive to keep it, we learn that we can't. When we don't keep it, we miss out on the life we hope to find there. We are trapped.

- *How does Scripture "make it clear" that we are locked up (Galatians 3:22)? Who can be set free from the control of sin?*

- *What is the key that can unlock us from the confinement of the law (v. 23)?*

If the law set clearly the boundaries of righteousness, it also made clear that no one is free from its demands. Who can love the Lord his God with all his heart, soul, and strength and his neighbor as himself? If the Jew fails in this regard, then so does the gentile. We are all shut in by these walls. There is no escape. There is only punishment and confinement for our crimes.

A helpful despair sets in—despair of finding righteousness in ourselves. We despair of our ability to obey the rules, our ability to meet the standard, our ability to avoid sin. That despair is where hope can be found, in the promise resting there quietly behind the law, beneath the law, older and more accessible than the law.

Bible scholar E. P. Sanders sums up this passage in this way: "God always intended to save by faith, apart from law. God gave the law, but he gave it in order that it would condemn all and thus prepare negatively for redemption on the basis of faith...The law was not given to make alive."[15]

Minding Children

- *What is the difference between a babysitter and a guardian? Which role did the law play before Jesus (v. 24)?*

- *What does a guardian do for the children under their care? How do the children respond to a guardian?*

- *When was the guardianship of the law terminated? Why? What changed that allowed its oversight to end (v. 25)?*

Paul writes that the law was given as a child-minder, a pedagogue. The Greek word here refers to a household servant whose job was to rear and discipline the master's children, often right alongside the household servants' own children. In a wealthy Roman household, newborns went to a wet nurse, then a nanny, and then a servant who taught them manners and socialization. Typically, this servant was a harsh disciplinarian using physical force and corporal punishment to keep the children in line. Roman children were often afraid of their pedagogues, and they obeyed out of fear for this parent-substitute. This, says Paul, is the role of the law.

Until maturity, until Christ, until faith, we needed a minder. We needed a harsh governess or a pedagogue who would keep us in line, fearful of condemnation and punishment. The law did this for us. It made the expected behavior clear. It laid out the punishments and corrections for disobedience. It stood over its charges with a scowl and a stick, ready to find the faults and punish them. This was the purpose of the law.

- *Whose arrival was anticipated by the law (vv. 16, 19, 22, 24)? What effects of the law would make anyone long for the Messiah?*

- *Where is the ultimate answer to our sin? Who is the righteousness that we need? Who is the hope for those in despair of ever being righteous? Who sets us free? Who brings us to maturity?*

- *What response to Jesus Christ frees people from the law (vv. 24–25)?*

Paul's Galatian readers needed to understand that the law was no longer binding on them, but neither was it worthless to them. Until Jesus came, the law was a stopgap to expose our transgressions, to show us the boundaries, to stimulate despair, to lock us up, to discipline us. All of this to prepare us for Christ, the fulfillment of the promise.

The law of Moses prepared the way from the promise of Abraham to its fulfillment in Christ.

 EXPERIENCE GOD'S HEART

- *What is the difference between sinfulness and impoliteness or irresponsibility? How do you determine which behaviors, attitudes, and thoughts are sinful?*

- *Have you ever realized that something you have done for a long time is actually a sin? How did you come to know this? Did someone teach you this? If so, what did they base it on?*

- *How do you feel about your ability to obey God? Does it come naturally or easily? Is it a battle?*

- *What do you think or feel when you fail to keep God's standard? What can you do about it?*

♥ SHARE GOD'S HEART

- *In general, do people think of themselves as sinners? Support your answer.*

- *Can they appreciate the gospel if they don't understand their sinful condition? What good is a rescue when there is no danger?*

- *Evangelist and Bible teacher D. L. Moody taught, "You've got to get people lost before you can get them saved." As you think about sharing your faith with a friend or relative, can you see the truth of this adage? How might you "get people lost"? What specific Scripture verses do you know that teach this truth?*

Talking It Out

1. Discuss other covenant-like legal agreements we use today. What happens when a new agreement is made while the old one remains in effect? Which one takes precedence?

2. Before we respond by faith to the good news of Jesus Christ, the law of Moses is busy addressing our transgressions, trapping us, and disciplining us. Talk about how the Old Testament rules still do this for us. Which of these roles seems most relevant to each group member?

LESSON 6

All God's Children

(Galatians 3:26–4:7)

For years, two brothers in their forties lived in a cave outside of Budapest, Hungary, selling scavenged junk to buy food and clothing. Then one day, a charity worker approached the make-shift lodgings of Zsolt and Geza Peladi to inform them that their grandmother had died in Germany. Since their estranged mother had already passed away, the brothers, along with a sister in America, were the direct heirs to their grandmother's $6.6 billion fortune. Geza told a Hungarian reporter, "We knew our mother came from a wealthy family, but she was a difficult person and severed ties with them, and then later abandoned us and we lost touch with her and our father until she eventually died."[16]

The Peladi brothers lived as paupers, sleeping in a cave, unaware of the riches that were already theirs. These brothers were entitled to the inheritance. They just didn't know it. They had never met their grandmother, so they didn't even know they were heirs to such wealth. They had never done anything to pursue that fortune. They did not work for a single penny of it. None of that mattered. All that counted was that they were part of the family.

False teachers told the Galatian believers that they were not the covenant people of God until they kept the law of Moses. Paul wrote to correct this lie and assure them they were in the family and, therefore, an invaluable inheritance was already theirs.

Children of the Father

- *Paul writes that the Galatians are true children of God "in Jesus Christ" (Galatians 3:26). Paul uses this phrase more than a hundred times in his letters. What does it mean to be "in Christ" (v. 27)?*

- *What individuals are clothed in Christ (v. 27)? How is being baptized like getting dressed?*

- *How does a person become a child of God (v. 26)? What if someone is already a Jew in covenant relationship with God through Moses (v. 28)? What if someone is a gentile who had never heard of the righteous requirements of the law? Does our social status matter? Our gender? Our ethnicity? Our poverty or wealth?*

- *Who are the members of Abraham's family who inherit the promise God made to them (v. 29)? Why might this statement surprise a first-century Jew?*

If the bold covenant-drawn line between Jew and non-Jew is irrelevant in Christ, how much more then is one's gender or social status? As children of God, slaves are equal to free people. As children of God, women are equal to men. All who believe in Christ are children of God and the offspring of Abraham.

Faith was the entrance door for Abraham, so it is the entrance door for all. If you are in Christ by faith, then you are like Abraham. Like Abraham, you are justified by faith. Like Abraham, you are an heir of the same promise he received. It came to Abraham by faith. It comes to us the same way.

THE EXTRA MILE

In second-century Christian practice, the metaphor of being clothed with Christ and his life was taken literally. Baptism candidates would strip off their old garments as they entered the baptism waters. As they emerged, more mature believers would cover them with a new white robe.[17]

The practice was a graphic illustration of what happens to everyone who puts his or her faith in Jesus. Before individuals believe, they stand before God in their old sin-stained self. Unclean, morally smudged, every good deed tainted with evil by their own unredeemed nature. The moment that an individual turns from his old life to embrace Christ, his heart is bathed and cleansed, and his nature is redeemed. Now he stands before God in the new, unblemished nature of Christ.

Here in Galatians, Paul identifies our spiritual clothing with our new identity. In other places, the metaphor speaks of the character that is developed as we cooperate with God's ongoing work in our lives. Either way, getting dressed and undressed describes the change that life in Christ makes. "If anyone is enfolded into Christ, he has become an entirely new person. All that is related to the old order has vanished. Behold, everything is fresh and new" (2 Corinthians 5:17).

- *Let's learn more about how Scripture uses this clothing metaphor. Fill out the following chart, paying special attention to what we should remove from our lives and what we should add and accept into our lives.*

	What we take off	What we put on
Romans 13:12–14		
Ephesians 6:11–18		
Colossians 3:5–14		
1 Peter 5:5–6		
Revelation 3:17–19		

Adopted by the Father

Paul returns to the pedagogue (guardian) analogy (Galatians 3:23–25). Before, he was focused on the law as the pedagogue, but now his focus is the clutch of children in the pedagogue's care.

- *Read 4:1–2. How is the father's child different from the other children? How is the treatment of the child the same as the treatment of the servants?*

- *Whom must the heir obey? How long does this arrangement last? Who determines when it ends?*

- *In this analogy, what is the guardian (3:24; 4:2–3)? Who is the master, the heir's father (3:26)? Who are the heirs (3:29; 4:7)?*

- *When did Jesus arrive on the scene (4:4)? In what two ways did Jesus identify with us in his birth?*

- *Why is it profound that God's Son had a mother like us?*

- *What was Jesus' relationship to the law when he came?*

- *What did the Son come to do (4:5)? What does it mean to be redeemed (3:14; 4:5)?*

- *How does redemption change our relationship to God?*

The world was underage for a long time. For over fifteen hundred years, the law of Moses ruled over God's people. During that time, there was very little obvious difference between a household servant and a child of the Master. Servant children and free children were alike under the rule of the pedagogue. That's how things were under the law of Moses.

Then, at the timing of the Father, when it was time for a more complete, mature treatment, Jesus came. He came as a human being, born of a woman. He came among the people who were living under the law of Moses. He came to bring us out from under the pedagogue's harsh oversight and into a new life of freedom in the Father's own family. He came as one of us, and he came for us. He came to redeem us. In his incarnation, Jesus identified with us so that we could identify with him by faith.

Heirs of the Father

When we think of adoption nowadays, we think of bringing an infant into our homes. For whatever circumstances, the child needs a stable home that his or her biological parents cannot or will not provide. Adoption, in these cases, means that the child will grow up knowing no other parents. The typical obligations of provision, protection, and direction fall to the adoptive parents. The right to this basic care belongs to the child. Inheritance is only an eventuality and not the primary concern.

In Bible times, adoption was very different. Babies were seldom taken in as adopted family members. Abandoned children were usually scooped up by slave traders, becoming part of the human trafficking trade. Adoption usually happened when a wealthy or royal person without heirs or without honorable heirs sought out an adult to inherit the estate or title. The adopted child's history was not changed, but his future was. The heir's upbringing may have been common, but his new status was noble at the choosing of the father.

Now everyone who was under the domination of the law can have the freedom of Jesus through adoption into God's family by faith.

- *What evidence do we have that we have been adopted as God's children (4:6)? Who indwells every child of God, and what does he teach us to call God?*

- *Paul uses both the Hebrew and the Greek terms for "father" in Galatians 4:6. Why is this significant in the context of Galatians?*

- *What were we before adoption (v. 7)? Since that is not our status anymore, what attitudes toward the old guardian should we discard?*

- *What future benefit of adoption awaits all God's children (v. 7)?*

 WORD WEALTH

When babies begin to talk, they make sounds that are easy to say. Usually, they babble simple one- or two-syllable words referring to their parents and grandparents, like mama or mum, papa or daddy, oma or opa. In most languages, there are more formal, harder-to-pronounce words, such as mother, father, and grandmother, but babies start with sounds and terms.

The word for "father" in Aramaic is *abba*. It is not a formal, complicated term, but neither is it babytalk. The same familiar term would be used by the simplest child and the most sophisticated adult. It was often used to convey intimacy but also respect for elders and teachers. Jesus almost certainly used this word when he taught his disciples to pray (Matthew 6:9; Luke 11:2), encouraging his disciples to approach God confidently from inside the family. This is the same way that Jesus the Son addressed God the Father when he prayed in the garden of Gethsemane (Mark 14:36).

In Galatians 4:6 and Romans 8:15, Paul pairs *Abba* with the Greek word *Pater*. In both passages, he wants his readers to understand that they are family. No matter their background, they were the dear children of God himself. He is equally *Abba* to Jewish believers and *Pater* to Greek believers. They belonged to the Father and, because of Jesus, could claim the relationship and inheritance that belong to his children.

We are not free because we broke out of spiritual jail. We are free because Jesus is free. The Spirit-filled, True Heir of God who pleases the Father in every way (Matthew 3:16–17) came into the world at God's appointed time. He lived a life like ours, died the death we deserved, and rose from the dead to give life to anyone who will believe. By his identifying with us in every way, we can identify with him as God's adopted children.

> The Word of God was made man, and He
> who was the Son of God became the Son of
> man, that man, having been taken into the
> Word, and receiving the adoption, might
> become the son of God.[18]
> The Son of God became a man to enable
> men to become sons of God.[19]

Now the Son's nature, his Spirit, his freedom, his grace, his covenant, his family, and his status as God's child and heir are granted to us by faith. We can call his Father our Father. His Abba is our Abba.

 EXPERIENCE GOD'S HEART

- *Read Galatians 3:26–4:7 again and review the changes that have taken place in anyone who has identified with Christ by faith. Then write a sentence about the change from your own point of view (e.g., "I am loved by the Father," "Jesus redeemed my life with his own").*

	Without Christ	In Christ
What characteristics determine our identity?		
My personal statement:		
How are we related to God?		
My personal statement:		
Who/what is our direct authority?		
My personal statement:		
What are our future spiritual prospects?		
My personal statement:		

♥ SHARE GOD'S HEART

- *Many of us have friends from different ethnic, cultural, religious, or social backgrounds. What are some of the obstacles to sharing the gospel across these divides?*

- *If these boundaries can be crossed in friendships, can they also be crossed in evangelism? What are the similarities between cross-cultural friendships and evangelism? What are the differences?*

- *How does knowing that the Christian church has always been a diverse community give you the confidence to communicate the gospel across such barriers?*

Talking It Out

1. It has been said that eleven o'clock on Sunday morning is the most segregated hour in North America, meaning that many churches are ethnically homogenous without the presence of minority groups. Talk about your own experiences in local churches. Have you ever been in the clear minority among other Christians because of your ethnicity, skin color, status, or gender? What do you think contributes to this separation?

2. How does Galatians 3:26–29 address these divisions in God's family?

3. Many Christians have committed to a lifelong ministry of adopting one or more children. Discuss together how this adoption changes the children, their status, and their futures. Talk about how it also changes the family too. Are these effects similar to the changes that happen when God adopts us as his own children?

LESSON 7

Losing Ground

(Galatians 4:8–20)

Paul and Barnabas were rejoicing when they returned to Antioch from Galatia (Acts 14:27). Their mission was successful. They preached the good news of God's grace to new hearers, largely gentiles devoted to an array of pagan deities, and many believed. The apostles established new churches and appointed new leaders to guide these fledgling congregations. From Paul's point of view, the new Galatian Christian movement was off to a great start. But great starts don't always lead to great finishes.

Every year on January 1, people the world over decide to make a fresh start. Every time we take down last year's calendar and put up the new one, we have the chance to do things differently, to break a bad habit or start a good one. A New Year, a new way of life. At least, that is the plan.

Half of the adults in the United States make New Year's resolutions, but only about 10 percent keep them for more than a few months.[20] The smoker, the gambler, the overeater, the big spender can all attest to this simple fact: starting off on the right foot doesn't guarantee that we will finish on it. A little temptation, a small stumble, a quick glance back at the old ways, and a good start comes to a bad end.

This was Paul's alarming realization. The Galatians were quickly turning away from his message of freedom to a religious idea just as enslaving as their old paganism. It would take more than resolve to set things right.

Back to Bondage

• *What did Paul's first readers serve before they had turned to the one true God (Galatians 4:8–9)?*

• *What new Jewish rituals were these former pagans practicing that gave Paul such great concern (v. 10)?*

• *What was Paul's response to what the Galatian believers were doing (v. 11)?*

The Greco-Roman world was awash in a sea of pagan religion. Galatian archaeological finds have uncovered shrines, temples, and inscriptions to dozens of pagan gods, from the popular mystery cults and emperor worship to such Greek gods as Artemis, Dionysus, Zeus, and Hermes.

The Galatian pagans' devotion to the Athenian deities was obvious to Paul and Barnabas on their first visit to Lystra (Acts 14:8–15). In that initial encounter, Paul called their pagan gods "worthless myths" (v. 15), and in his letter to the Galatians, Paul said that these "powers that be" were "nothing compared to God" (Galatians 4:8). The falseness and worthlessness of their gods, however, did not keep people from being enslaved to them. While not truly gods, they were still powerful, dangerous, and demanding. That's why the gospel was so necessary, to set the Galatians straight and set them free.

But now freedom was slipping away! The same demonic powers that held them in bondage as pagans were taking advantage of their gullible spiritual immaturity. They were reasserting their dominance over the Galatians through the anti-grace message of the Judaizing false preachers.

Could the God-initiated law of Moses become a bondage to these gentile converts? Paul teaches that it could. Any reliance on their own works erased the grace in the good news. The obligations of law-keeping would undermine the freedom of the gospel. Instead of trusting in pagan rituals and myths for eternal life, they were turning to embrace Jewish rituals to complete their new religion. Either way, human effort and religious rites were bondage and no legitimate alternative to the saving grace of God in Christ.

Their old religion made them slaves; gospel faith made them sons. Their old religion kept them in bondage, dominated and oppressed by false deities; gospel faith brought them into the family, to be known and loved by Abba God. Adherence to religious law, even good laws, would steal their freedom in Christ. How could they even consider turning back to bondage?

We imagine that those first-century Christians were uniquely tempted to fall away from grace in this way. However, a glance at the modern Christian movement reveals millions who are vigilant about ritual observances without knowing God or being known by God. They are driven to perform but never drawn into friendship with God. Religious obligations wholly define their spiritual experience. Sometimes they feel guilty when they miss a church service, but they do not know the joy of daily walking with God. Satisfied with a weekly observance or an annual attendance, they never find their new belonging in the household of Father God.

Incident of Illness

- *After such teaching and scolding, what terms of tenderness does Paul use to address his readers (Galatians 4:12)? What does this say about his attitude toward them, even in their foolishness?*

- *What other phrases in verses 12–16 demonstrate the deep affection shared between Paul and the Galatian Christians?*

Paul's health condition referred to here is not described in Acts.[21] Indeed, there is no reference to any sickness among the apostles in that earliest historical account. Because this illness is not part of the narrative, we do not know its exact nature or how it led to ministry among the Galatians. However, there are some clues.

- *Compare Galatians 4:15 and 6:11. What sort of ailment do these verses indicate Paul had?*

- *Did Paul's infirmity keep the Galatians from receiving his message? What kind of reception did they give him initially?*

- *How had their affection for Paul changed (4:15–16)?*

🛣 THE EXTRA MILE

To listen to some teachers, you might think that there should never be an illness among Christians. After all, didn't Jesus promise that praying with faith the size of a mustard seed would always yield the desired outcome (Matthew 17:20)? Didn't James write that the prayer of faith will make the sick person well (James 5:15–16)? Based on these passages, can't we always expect healing when we pray?

These assumptions eventually collide with reality, not only in our own day but in the early church as well. Paul had performed many healings, but even his ministry had unresolved illnesses. Read the following passages. Take note of who was ill and what the circumstances were. If Paul offered a solution for the illness, what was it? What do you conclude from each example?

Passage	Patient	Counsel	Conclusion
1 Corinthians 11:27–32			
2 Corinthians 12:7–10			
Philippians 2:25–30			
1 Timothy 5:23			

Devious Division

As the Galatians were influenced by the false gospel of the Judaizing preachers, their opinion of faraway Paul was changing. Separated from the apostles who had introduced them to the true gospel, their defenses were down, their convictions were confused, and they were vulnerable. They began to lose their tenderness toward Paul, and some even saw him as a spiritual enemy. This was the purposeful strategy of these false teachers.

- *What steps were Paul's enemies taking to turn the hearts of the Galatians away from the gospel (Galatians 4:17)?*

- *What did Paul say was much better to strive for (v. 18)?*

The Judaizers were in Galatia, and Paul was far away. They could criticize and attack Paul with impunity in his absence, and he could not defend himself. By the time he heard about the troubles there, the Judaizers had already planted doubts in the minds of the Galatians about the legitimacy of Paul's ministry and message. Instead of seeing Paul as a spiritual parent to them, they had begun to see him as an enemy.

- *What metaphor does Paul use to describe his effort and anguish on behalf of the Galatians (v. 19)?*

- *How does Paul describe the Galatians' maturity in Christ (v. 19)?*

- *What does he wish he could do and why (v. 20)?*

A healthy start is not enough; a healthy finish is the goal. Spiritual conversion is a good initial start, but spiritual maturity is the finish line. Paul labored for the Galatians' sound doctrine and maturity in Christ. He had planted the seed of the gospel in them. They were in the process of maturing when the false gospel was introduced. Now Paul, separated from them, worried that this process might end in spiritual miscarriage, and he was deeply disturbed over this.

What would happen to these vulnerable young churches? Would they heed this urgent warning of the apostle who loved them so deeply? Would they finish as well as they had started?

💠 EXPERIENCE GOD'S HEART

- *Many new believers go through periods of doubt and confusion when they encounter new teachings they weren't prepared for. Have you been distracted or misled by a new teaching? Why were you vulnerable to it? What got you back on track?*

- *It seems Paul wasn't miraculously healed from the ailment that provided the opportunity for the Galatians to care for him. A miracle might have short-circuited that ministry. Have you experienced physical healing? Have you prayed for healing, for yourself or others, without being healed? Was there any long-term spiritual impact from that healing or ungranted request?*

9 SHARE GOD'S HEART

- *Certainly, finishing well requires perseverance and focus, but a little encouragement goes a long way. Can you think of anyone in your circle of believers who started well but seems to be flagging? Maybe he or she has become distracted. Maybe this person is trapped in an eddy of doubt. Maybe the old life is pulling hard on this individual. Take some time to pray for this person and then find a way to encourage him or her in the way of Christ.*

- *The Christian message is not merely one of doctrine; it is an invitation into the family of God. Through faith in Christ, the Lord is our Abba Father, and we are brothers and sisters in his family. How might this invitation to the family affect the way you share the good news with others?*

Talking It Out

1. Discuss your past New Year's resolutions. How did you do?
   Did any of those commitments lead to permanent change?
   If so, which ones? What made the difference between
   permanence and temporary adherence?

2. Many parents feel the anguish of Paul when their young
   adult children leave home. Without parents or lifelong
   friendships around them, their children make questionable
   choices. All Mom and Dad can do is watch helplessly from
   a distance and pray. Talk about this situation with your
   small group. Have you ever been in that situation with
   your children? Were you that child? Can you relate to the
   frustration of Paul for the Galatians?

LESSON 8

Who's Your Mama?

(Galatians 4:21–31)

If you have a dog, is it a lurcher? Lurchers have no specific recognized pedigree. They are the result of mating a sighthound, like a whippet, a greyhound, or a wolfhound, with a dog of a working breed, like a collie or a terrier. The sighthound lineage makes lurchers exceedingly fast, and the working dog lineage makes them clever. One Irish family owns a lurcher, and she has impressed the locals with her gentleness. Their approval rises even more when they learn that her mother—a well-trained, docile, and friendly Irish wolfhound cross—is an animal they respect and love.

"Fine lurcher you have there. What's her breeding?"

"A bit of whippet, greyhound, wolfhound, Bedlington terrier, and a handful of others," the family will say. "And she's a daughter to Io."

"Ah," they will say, "*that's* why you have such a lovely lurcher."[22]

Observers know by instinct what breeders know by profession. The nature of the pup springs from the nature of its mother.

In Galatians 4:21–31, Paul returns to the use of analogy to explain his message of grace. This time he uses an example from history, an analogy about pedigree, spiritual natures, mothers, and their offspring.

THE BACKSTORY

We have already seen how Abraham believed God's promise to give him a son and how that faith in God's promise was the basis of Abraham's righteousness. This historical analogy comes directly from three episodes in the life of Abraham that followed his justification by faith. Because the details of the story are so important for the analogy that Paul uses, it's important that you read the background passages and answer the following questions.

• *Genesis 16:1–16*

What two women are central to this story? What was the status of each woman in Abram's household?

What steps did Abram take to "help" God keep his promise?

How did conflict arise between the women and Abram?

How did the women treat one another?

Who ran away from the family?

What did God tell the runaway woman to do? What did he promise her about her unborn child?

How old was Abram when her child was born?

• *Genesis 18:1–15*

Who appeared to Abraham (Abram's new name)?

What promise did the visitors give to Abraham that day?

Who was listening in while Abraham heard the promise? Did the listening person believe the overheard promise? Why or why not?

- *Genesis 21:1–14*

> *How did God keep his promise to Abraham? Why was keeping this promise such a miracle?*

> *How old was Abraham when Sarah's child was born? How many years had passed since the birth of Hagar's child?*

> *What conflict was evident between the two children?*

> *How did Abraham address the household conflict?*

The Mothers Explained

These are the relevant facts on which Paul's motherhood analogy is based. He tells us that, although this story is factual history, there are figurative principles to be drawn from it. From this history, Abraham's family was meant to show us the contrast between slavery and freedom, natural life and supernatural life, law and grace.

- *Which woman was free (Galatians 4:21–22)? How was she related to Abraham?*

- *Which conception occurred purely through human effect (v. 23)? Which woman was promised a miraculous child?*

After reviewing the details of the backstory, Paul begins to spell out his illustration. He does it through a series of contrasts between the two women, Hagar and Sarah. Interestingly, he never mentions Sarah by name, perhaps because she was so well known that it was unnecessary.

- *How is the old covenant like Hagar (v. 24)? Based on our study of Galatians so far, did the covenant of Moses enslave? How?*

- *Who does Paul imply are Hagar's children? What does "the earthly Jerusalem" represent (v. 25)?*

The explanation so far points to those who trust in the old covenant. Mostly, this refers to Jews who have not embraced the good news of their Messiah, who are still hoping that their efforts to follow Moses will be adequate for salvation. But it also certainly points to those who are tacking obedience to the law on to the gospel. Both groups are enslaved and, worse, advocating for others to be enslaved.

This analogy would have been incredibly offensive to the Judaizing reader. They believed that they were the true descendants of Sarah and Isaac. They were certain that they were the people of promise. Surely, they were not the slave-children of Hagar!

Paul reminded his readers of the geography of the law of Moses. The law was given to the Hebrews at Sinai in the land of the Ishmaelites, the region where Hagar and Ishmael went when Sarah sent them away. Paul was figuratively calling the Judaizers Ishmaelites.

Even if they refused to take that ethnic connection to heart, Paul wouldn't let them off the hook. He tied Jerusalem, their beloved capital city, the center of Sinai law-keeping, to bondage. When Paul wrote the letter to the Galatians, Jerusalem was under the thumb of foreign Roman occupiers. In either case, he was calling law-keepers slaves.

Incidentally, this is the same quarrel that Jesus had with the Jews in John 8:31–47. When the Lord told his audience how to be set free, they objected that they could not possibly be slaves. They were ethnically the children of Abraham! Jesus explained that, of course, they were slaves. Their true slave-master was sin itself, their true father was the devil, and they could never understand truth because they would not listen to Jesus. The way to be set free from their slavery was not through Moses or some ancient physical connection to Abraham; it was simply to be Jesus' disciple. It was to receive the truth by faith. By the time Jesus was finished speaking about this, his listeners had picked up rocks to stone him (v. 59). Paul repeats this same offensive message here.

 THE EXTRA MILE

After Jacob's family went down to Egypt in Genesis 48, they prospered and multiplied. By the time the book of Exodus begins, these immigrants were overwhelming their hosts, and Pharaoh was afraid. He tried to limit their numbers, and when that didn't work, he enslaved them (Exodus 1).

Israel's bondage was so severe that they cried out to God for deliverance. He called Moses to go and announce freedom. The effect wasn't immediate. Pharaoh didn't want to part with the free labor. But after ten plagues, including the loss of their firstborn children, the Egyptians let the Hebrews go. From that point on, the theme of bondage and freedom seasons the Scriptures.

- *Look up these passages about slavery. Who is the slave? Who is the master? What are the circumstances? Is the slavery mentioned physical or spiritual? Is freedom offered?*

Slavery, Freedom, and Service

Text	Insights
Exodus 6:2–8	
Deuteronomy 7:7–11	
Jeremiah 34:8–20	
Mark 10:42–45	
John 8:31–40	
Romans 6:15–23	
Hebrews 2:14–18	
2 Peter 2:17–22	

# THE BACKSTORY

As Paul turns to the other woman in Galatians 4:26, he quotes from the great Hebrew prophet Isaiah. The prophecy comes from Isaiah 54:1 and follows right on the heels of Isaiah 53, the great chapter of the Surrendered Servant. Isaiah's prophecy describes the life of this matchless man who came to live among us.

- *How did we respond to God's servant when he grew up among us (Isaiah 53:3)?*

- *How did he help us with our troubles (vv. 4, 6)? What did he endure for our sins (v. 5)?*

- *How are we like sheep (v. 6)? In what ways do we stray and go our own way?*

- *How was he like a lamb when he suffered for our sakes (v. 7)?*

- *What was the cause of his death and his being stricken (v. 8)?*

- *Where was he buried when he died (v. 9)? How was this prophecy fulfilled (Matthew 27:57–60)?*

- *What had God's Servant done to deserve this severe treatment (Isaiah 53:9)?*

The sinless Surrendered Servant endured much for our sakes. By God's sovereign plan, he bore our sin and guilt. The judgment that we deserved fell on him. He died and was buried along with the wicked, but he was also resurrected to see the light of life (see Isaiah 53:10).

Through the knowledge of his atoning sacrifice, many people are made righteous (v. 11). This is the very heart of Paul's message to the Galatians. Therefore, it is no coincidence that Paul takes his readers to Isaiah 54:1 to highlight the children set free by the new covenant.

Back to the Mothers and Their Children

• *How does Isaiah 54:1 relate to the story of Sarah and Hagar?*

• *How are the converted Galatians like Isaac (Galatians 4:28)?*

The throng of people rescued and atoned for by God's Servant are the figurative children of Sarah. They are not born in the natural way. They are born again supernaturally by the promise of God. They are a vast and growing number, including the Galatians. And just as the son of Sarah faced jeers and persecution from within her household, it was not easy going for the new Galatian church either.

- *Who persecuted Isaac? Who persecuted the new Galatian Christians (Galatians 4:29)?*

- *How did God deal with the family conflict between Sarah and Hagar, Ishmael and Isaac?*

- *How did Paul want the Galatians to deal with the Judaizers (v. 30)?*

- *Who is free? Who is enslaved (v. 31)?*

The Galatian churches were faced with a choice. They could go on tolerating the false teachers in their midst, or they could evict them. If they allowed their influence to continue, confusion, persecution, and slavery would also continue. Using the historical account of Sarah and Hagar, Paul urged them to separate from these perverters of the true gospel. Only then could the free children of the Promise, justified by faith and not works, grow up in God's household unhindered.

Why This Analogy?

Jews reading Paul's letter would have known well the details of the Abraham-Sarah-Hagar story. They would not have come to the same conclusions as Paul, of course. It was not obvious to them that they were enslaved by their human effort to obey the rules of the covenant. They would *never* have considered themselves the children of Hagar. Still, they would have been familiar with the history.

Gentiles reading this letter would have been clueless. Ordinarily, gentiles did not know the historical or cultural details or the significance of these episodes in Abraham's life. They would have had to search the Scriptures to learn this backstory, just as we have. New gentile believers were the primary audience for this letter. So why did Paul use this analogy at all?

Probably, Paul uses this story to explain things because his opponents had used the same story to muddle things.[23] The Ishmael and Isaac story was a well-known foundational text in first-century synagogues. It seems the Judaizers were teaching it as something like this:

> God's people have always been physically
> related to Abraham through Isaac.
> Everyone else is outside the covenant
> promises like Ishmael. Jews have a free
> woman for their mother. We received
> God's direct revelation of the law at Mount
> Sinai. We have circumcision to confirm all
> this. Surely, following Jesus, the Jewish
> Messiah, changes none of these things.
> Gentiles might be welcome now, but they
> still must come in a Jewish way!

In this interpretation of the Judaizers, even faith in Jesus didn't get gentiles *all* the way into the family. They still had some Jewish steps to take. With the Galatians so quickly succumbing to this message, Paul revisited this text and gave it a Spirit-inspired clarification. His explanation showed the gentile Christians that this essential text is misunderstood when it places faith in anything but God's promises. The legitimate children of Abraham are in the family because of faith and *nothing* else.

As you review the principles illustrated by Abraham's family, fill in the following contrasts between the old covenant and the new as Paul describes them.

Household Analogy of Two Covenants (Galatians 4:21–31)			
Covenant 1	**Element**	**Reference**	**Covenant 2**
	Child		
	Nature		
	Mother		
	Means		
	Covenant		
	Geography		

Your Pedigree

What is *your* pedigree? Ultimately, the answer to this question is not about ethnicity. It's not the bloodline going back to Sarah that makes you a child of the free woman. That, too, is the natural pedigree. And it isn't striving to keep the rules of the first covenant that sets us free. Those are just ordinary, non-miraculous human accomplishments.

To be a child of promise, a figurative free child of Sarah, you must follow Father Abraham's example. You must believe the promise of God. The promise of sins atoned for and sorrows carried miraculously. The promise of the eternal through the Surrendered Servant. These things are supernatural, more than any one of us can accomplish without God.

Following Jesus and receiving his truth by faith is the only way to freedom. Every other way leaves you a slave.

 EXPERIENCE GOD'S HEART

- *In the backstory of Abraham and Sarah, there is a range of faith responses. Abraham believes the promise, but Sarah laughs. They know God's promise must be true, but they scheme to help him keep it. What is your faith pattern like? Is it consistently improving, or is it a series of ups and downs? Does your own confidence in God waver? What helps you believe?*

- *Reread Isaiah 53 about the Surrendered Servant whom we know to be Jesus. Do you realize that every time this Scripture passage reads "we" and "us," you are included? Read each verse out loud, personalizing it as you go along. For example, instead of saying, "He was wounded for our transgressions," say, "He was wounded for my transgressions." Use this time to praise God for what he has done through his Son to deliver us from the curse of sin.*

- *Are you among the countless multitudes rescued and atoned for by God's Servant, the figurative children of Sarah (Galatians 4:27)? Have you recognized what Jesus did about your sin? Have you put your faith in him? Have you believed God's promise of miraculous new birth? If not, put your trust in him today.*

❤ SHARE GOD'S HEART

- *Everyone who believes that their behavior or their participation in religion makes them righteous remains part of the slave family. Only faith in Christ makes a person free. How do you feel about sharing the gospel with people who already belong to a religion?*

- *If the Son sets you free, you are free indeed (Galatians 5:1). When you talk about Jesus to others, do you sound as if you are presenting a message of liberation? If not, why?*

Talking It Out

1. When false teachers arise in the Christian community, how does Paul imply we should deal with them?

2. Discuss why it is hard to reprimand and oust false teachers in contemporary churches.

3. What damage is done when we fail to challenge and remove false teachers from our churches?

LESSON 9

Fragile Freedom

(Galatians 5:1–12)

Having established that Judaizers were slaves outside Abraham's family of faith, Paul pressed forward into his message of radical gospel freedom.

- *Who has set us free by faith (Galatians 5:1)? What should we do to protect our freedom?*

- *Can you think of any reasons that a freed prisoner would want to return to prison? If so, jot them down.*

The whole point of a jailbreak is to live in freedom on the outside. Getting out to go back inside is an utter waste of effort!

In Alexandre Dumas' novel *The Count of Monte Cristo*, Edmond Dantès was unjustly condemned to the inescapable Château d'If prison. After six years of solitary confinement, Dantès was attempting suicide by hunger strike when he heard the scratch, scratch, scratching of metal against stone. At first, he mistook the noise for a rat and then a rescuer. The draught of liberty was enough to banish his despair. From his own side, he began to pick away at the barrier. A few days later, he was conversing with a fellow prisoner.

While the sound of another human voice brought fresh hope to Dantès, it meant complete failure to his new companion, Faria. "I have made a mistake owing to an error in my plans. I took the wrong angle, and have come out fifteen feet from where I intended. I took the wall you are mining for the outer wall of the fortress...but now all is lost."

Faria had spent years scraping his way through fifty feet of solid stone to get out. Now, when he thought freedom was at hand, he discovered that he had merely tunneled into another prison cell. To hope so much, to work so hard, to come so far, only to continue in bondage was nothing short of tragic.

Paul feels the same about the Galatians, only more so. The message they needed for freedom was theirs. The plan was clear. So they believed the gospel, and their slavery was ended. They were on their way, but then someone steered them wrong. They were making a U-turn and burrowing back into their old cell.

A Worthless Christ?

Is Christ not enough (Galatians 5:2)? Even just reading that question seems blasphemous. Paul meant to offend by the suggestion, to shock the Galatians out of their complacency. They were choosing a path based on human effort rather than the grace of God. We cannot walk somewhere and drive at the same time. If we walk, the car is useless to us. Likewise, we cannot rely on the unearned favor of God for salvation while also trying to earn salvation through our own righteous efforts. To choose one is to *not* choose the other.

- *What evidence is there in verse 2 that Paul's audience was largely made up of gentiles?*

- *How could the One who should mean everything to them be inadequate for them (v. 2)?*

- *Why would getting circumcised oblige someone to keep the whole law of Moses (vv. 3–4)?*

- *Why does trying to be justified by the law separate us from Jesus (v. 4)?*

- *Describe grace in your own words. Why do faith and grace go together?*

- *When will those who are saved by faith be fully righteous (v. 5)?*

In our last lesson, we saw how Paul's enemies wanted to alienate the Galatians from him and others who could reinforce the true gospel. Here we see the even graver threat that the Galatians might be alienated (cut off) from Christ himself. Reliance on any religious effort will, by necessity, sever your connection with Jesus. If he is your salvation, you need no works to earn it. If you still believe you do, he is not your salvation. If you believe that good works make you righteous, what room is there for grace?

On the other hand, if justification is a gift, we can rest in that connection we have in Jesus. Our identification with him, our inseparable closeness to him, makes us righteous immediately before God and gradually in practice. At the culmination of history, our connection to Jesus will make us completely righteous forever.

Therefore, outward religious signs are useless. The only outward evidence we need are the Spirit-induced acts of love that come from our genuine faith.

- *What about Jewish Christians who were circumcised as infants? Are they disqualified from salvation through Jesus (v. 6)?*

- *Compare Galatians 5:6 with 1 Corinthians 7:18–20. What principle does Paul teach regarding any individual circumcision?*

Tripped Up

At the Los Angeles Olympics in 1984, American Mary Decker was heavily favored to win the three-thousand-meter run. For the final laps, Zola Budd, representing Great Britain, caught up and ran side-by-side with the presumed champion. In the final stretch, Budd moved ahead of Decker and tried to cut in, leading to a dramatic collision. That split-second mistake wiped out more than just eight minutes of one race. It derailed years of training and ended both athletes' hopes for gold. Decker never even finished the race.

- *It doesn't take much. A little stumble can take you out of the race. What other small influence does Paul mention (Galatians 5:9)?*

- *Given what Paul says, how much false gospel does it take to be disastrous? How much trusting in works erases grace?*

- *Who does Paul believe will lead his readers back to the truth? And what does he think will happen to the false teachers (v. 10)?*

- *Paul doesn't name his opponents, but he describes them and their work in four different ways (vv. 7–12). What are they?*

)

)

)

)

- *Who is clearly not the source of this false gospel (v. 8)?*

Persecution for Preaching

- *How can we know that Paul's gospel was opposed to the law-keepers' message (v. 11)? How would things be different if Paul's preaching agreed with what the false teachers presented?*

By this point in his letter, it's obvious that Paul adamantly opposed adding works to faith. However, it appears that some of the false teachers may have suggested that Paul endorsed their message. This would have influenced them greatly. After all, he was the one who first brought the good news of Jesus to them.

Would they drive him from town if they agreed? Would they have pursued him from town-to-town stirring up trouble if he preached the same message? Of course not!

The Unkindest Cut

When Shakespeare wrote about Brutus' sword giving Julius Caesar the "most unkindest cut," he was referring to Brutus' treachery. This friend, Caesar's traitorous false friend, conspired with Caesar's enemies to stab him to death. The wound came from inside the circle of trust.

In this short passage in Galatians, there are repeated references to cutting. Obviously, there is the topic of circumcision, a small cut to male genitals (5:2–3, 6, 11). There is the inevitable alienation from the Lord Jesus when we embrace a salvation that doesn't depend on him (v. 4). Finally, there is the most colorful reference of all. Paul wishes that those who insist on circumcision would perform a radical circumcision, that they would go the whole way and emasculate themselves (v. 12; see the TPT study note on this verse).

These Judaizers were presumed to be friends and family, but they were doing some serious intimate damage to the church. By pushing the works-based ceremonial righteousness of circumcision, these false friends were cutting new Christians off from Christ and cutting in on their path of grace. Paul's imprecation is that these false friends would deliver the unkindest cut to themselves.

Paul began this passage with the command to stand firm against returning to "the bondage of our past" (v. 1). It is the defensive posture of a hero facing his enemies. We have been given good news, the message that Jesus has accomplished all we need for justification before God. Simple trust in him will save us and even mature us. We mislead ourselves and others when we forget this. Trust in our own righteous behavior undermines the gospel.

Furthermore, the freedom Jesus gave us is at stake. He set us free so that we would live unencumbered by obligatory ceremony and rules. He set us free so that we would never again be trapped in the notion that God's love and favor depend on our behavior. He set us free so that we would be confident through our connection with Christ himself. He set us free to rest in our identification with him.

The gospel is a radical message like no other. All other attempts to get to God burden adherents with codes and rules, cultural signifiers and religious rituals. They demand obedience from the believer. The Christian gospel, on the other hand, begins with the awareness that behavior can never get us to righteousness. It depends on nothing more than the faithfulness of Christ.

All religious and even irreligious systems take offense at the gospel's radical message. That's why Christians who preach the gospel in keeping with Galatians find persecution and pressure wherever they go. Still, the freedom offered in Jesus is worth the fight, and this freedom must be defended if we mean to keep it.

🚦 THE EXTRA MILE

The Bible is full of military and spiritual conflicts. From Joshua at Jericho to David facing Goliath to Paul confronting the Judaizers, there are fights worth fighting. The tactics for these battles are varied, but each one demonstrates the power and justice of God.

- *Below are several passages that tell God's people in various ways to stand firm. Like Paul's instructions to the Galatians to "firmly refuse to go back" (5:1), these examples urge God's warriors to take a defensive stance, sometimes even an offensive one, if we want to experience the victory of God. Look up each passage and then write down what you learn about the setting, the stakes, and the result.*

Text	Setting	Stakes	Result
Exodus 14:9–14, 21–31			
2 Chronicles 20:15–25			
Matthew 24:3–14			
1 Corinthians 15:56–58			
1 Corinthians 16:13–14			
Ephesians 6:10–18			
James 5:7–11			
1 Peter 5:8–11			

⚘ EXPERIENCE GOD'S HEART

- *Being set free implies potential or experienced bondage. Without the possibility of oppression, the idea of freedom barely registers as the treasure it truly is. Think of the things that the gospel sets us free from. Better still, maybe there are some specific things from which you personally have been freed. Make a list and thank God for each freedom.*

- *The Galatians were free, but they were choosing to think and behave like they were enslaved. They were being drawn back into unnecessary obligations. Have you adopted any religious obligations that the gospel does not require? How can these obligations distract from the simple message of grace?*

♥ SHARE GOD'S HEART

- *One reason the gospel is so hard to defend is that its message is counterintuitive. How can our righteousness have nothing to do with our behavior? This can keep us from sharing God's heart with others, but is it really that unreasonable? Can you think of any other situations or relationships where the love is unconditional or the favor unearned? What are they, and how do they compare to the gospel of grace?*

Talking It Out

1. In the *Avengers* films, there are multiple moments when the team is defending against a horde of enemies. They stand back-to-back, each of them using their skills and marvelous abilities to stand firm, to hold the line. Talk about how your small group or church could defend the gospel together against spiritual opposition.

2. Find a website or print publication about the persecuted church.[24] Read one or two of the stories. Then talk about how the persecution that these brothers and sisters endure results from the fact that they refuse to compromise the good news. Discuss how the persecution would end immediately if they abandoned their message of righteousness by faith in Jesus alone. Answer this together: Is the gospel worth the personal cost?

LESSON 10

The Fruit Fight

(Galatians 5:13–26)

Rising above US 50, eight miles west of Canon City, CO, is Skyline Drive.[25] Built in 1903 by the labor of sixty inmates of the local state prison, this scenic roadway follows the ridge of a hog-back mountain with stunning views of the Arkansas River Valley. While the road is maintained and paved, it has no guardrails. At various points along the three-mile-long stretch of narrow, winding road, there are only sheer cliffs on either side. Furthermore, there is no way to turn back if the fear of heights gets the better of you. It is a one-way road.

On Skyline Drive, veering to the right might result in a tumble of eight hundred feet to the bottom of the ridge. Veering to the left is just as dangerous. Erring in one direction or the other would be disastrous. The only safe route is straight up the center of the road.

Whenever we Christians take our spiritual freedom seriously, there are two equally dangerous errors to avoid. To the one side, there is the error of *legalism*. Over this cliff lies the proliferation of religious rules, self-righteousness, judgment of others, perpetual anxiety of falling short, and eternal insecurity about salvation. To the other side, there is the error of *libertinism*. Over this cliff lies self-indulgence, perpetual immaturity, insensitivity to conscience, judgment and judgmentalism, and self-doubt over our lack of spiritual growth. Christians often veer off one side to avoid the hazards on the side.

From the start of this letter to the Galatians, Paul has been railing against the first error. He has shown us the fatal flaw of trusting in anything but faith for our salvation. He has shown us how adding any demand for works to the message of grace distorts the gospel.

But at this point, we are likely to ask predictable questions about the second error. If my salvation does not depend on my works of righteousness, can't I just sin? If we are justified before God by faith alone, what role is left for good works? If we gain nothing from striving to keep the law, does it even matter how we behave? In other words, why should we be good? Someone could say, "I love to sin; God loves to forgive. What a beautiful arrangement!"

Paul expected this response in his letter to the Romans. After carefully laying out the principles of justification by faith alone, he imagined his reader's retort, "So what do we do, then? Do we persist in sin so that God's kindness and grace will increase?... Should we sin to our hearts' content since there's no law to condemn us anymore?" To both questions Paul answered, "What a terrible thought!" (Romans 6:1–2, 15).[26]

We should note that solid preaching of the pure good news of God's grace will *always* lead to this question: What is the place for good works? When we declare that righteous deeds *cannot* achieve a righteous standing with God, people will ask it. When we proclaim that we are free from the burden of keeping the law for salvation, people will ask it. Removing the possibility of this response removes the possibility of grace. Paul acknowledged this dilemma in his revolutionary gospel of freedom and offered a revolutionary solution in his ethics of freedom.

• *What is the goal of the Lord's calling on us (Galatians 5:13)?*

- *What do you think of when you hear the word freedom? Is it freedom from something? Is it freedom for some purpose? Is it the freedom to do something?*

- *What potential danger does Paul see in this freedom he has been teaching (v. 13)?*

- *How should Christians use the freedom we have in Christ (vv. 13–14)? What motive should prompt our behavior now? How is that different from following rules?*

- *What happens to our relationships with others if we wrongly apply the principle of gospel freedom (v. 15)? How might we treat one another if we forget to love?*

New Servanthood

The New Testament message of freedom is as easily distorted as the Old Testament standard of righteousness. Maybe at the mention of freedom, we think, "Hooray! No boundaries! I can do whatever I want to do!" Freedom *from* sin can be twisted into freedom *to* sin. Paul recognized this distortion and pushed back hard. If we indulge ourselves, we misuse our God-given, Christ-purchased freedom. We make the opposite but equally dangerous mistake of the Judaizers.

To guard against a self-indulgent, self-exalting, self-centered lifestyle that dishonors Christ and destroys others, we humbly serve other people. We put others ahead of ourselves. When others become our focus, when our service is gladly offered to others, when we desire and do what is best for others, we will not misuse our new-found freedom. Instead of squandering our freedom on our own desires, we can lavish great love on others. We no longer need to put in the effort, time, and concentration to meet a religious standard. That kind of slaving away is behind us. Jesus already did that on our behalf. His righteousness is given freely to those who believe. Now we can freely and self-sacrificially give our effort, time, and concentration to tending the needs of others.

 THE EXTRA MILE

Jesus lived a life fully devoted to the needs of others. He modeled the freedom to serve. Look up the following passages to see what the Bible says about our Servant King.

Text	Insights
Isaiah 42:1	
Matthew 20:25–28	
Mark 6:31–34	
Mark 9:33–35	
John 13:12–17	
Philippians 2:7–8	

New Standard

So how do we know what good things to do? Do we run back to the law of Moses in desperation for some objective standard of morality? Do we elevate the very law for sanctification that we are no longer obliged to keep for our justification? Lest we think we must return to the Old Testament law of Moses to get our description of an ethical life, Paul spelled out the radically simple ethics of the New Testament.

In place of the 636 old covenant commands, we essentially have one: love one another as you love yourself. This is the new Christian ethic that supersedes the Mosaic law. It is deeper, broader, and more enduring than the law.

The love ethic of Christianity is deeper because it is the grounding of all the human-directed laws of the Old Testament. In the Ten Commandments, for example, dishonoring parents, theft, murder, adultery, lying, and coveting are all violations of the love ethic. Someone who loves his neighbor as himself will not do these things. Love makes the requirements of the law irrelevant. That is why Jesus called this the second greatest commandment, behind only an all-encompassing love for God. He taught us, "Contained within these commandments to love you will find all the meaning of the Law and the Prophets" (Matthew 22:40).

The love ethic is broader because it is not exclusive to a particular people group. The law of Moses was given to Israel. It was God's prescription for a nation living in submission to him. It was the way they could show that they were his people and he was their God. It was the detailed ethic for a specific ethnic group. The love ethic, on the other hand, is applicable to all people groups. A Jewish Christian can keep it, but so can the Congolese, the Korean, the Apache, and the Dutchman.

The love ethic is more enduring because it will always be our ethic. At the culmination of history, when all other rules and codes are unnecessary, we will still love. We will love others unhindered by sin or selfishness. We will not want to do any of the things that the law forbade because love will permeate us and all we do.

The love ethic is Jesus' new command for his people, not because it was never mentioned before but because it is the ultimate law of the new covenant. The love ethic isn't primarily a restraint against unloving things, but it frees us to love in creative and unexpected ways that the law of Moses never imagined. Because of love, we forgive offenders, we pray for those who persecute us, we give without expecting anything in return, we lay down our lives for one another, and we care for the fatherless and the widow. Because of love, we can serve others rather than serving ourselves.[27]

New Guide

We should not imagine that we are alone in figuring out the implications of the love ethic. God's help for this new life is personal and supernatural. Jesus promised us "another Savior" for this life of faith.

- *Read John 14:15–18, 26. Who is this other Savior? What things did Jesus promise that this other One would do for us?*

- *What is the supernatural key to avoiding the self-indulgent distortion of freedom (Galatians 5:16)?*

- *Paul mentions a conflict that occurs as we live the new life. Describe the two sides and their goals (vv. 16–17).*

- *Why can the Christian live an upright life without the oversight or directives of the law (v. 18)?*

The personal, divine presence of God is real. God the Holy Spirit lives in every one of us who believes. He will show us the way to go (Psalm 32:8; Isaiah 30:21), so our obligation is to walk in that direction. When we follow his leading, we live holy lives. He is the *Holy* Spirit, after all. With the Holy Spirit's ministry, we do not need to observe the law. A Christian adhering to the love ethic under the direction of the Holy Spirit will live a godly life.

In some ways, this is easier than following a written code. What do we do in a given situation? What does God require of us? The law is not always clear in every situation of life. Now, in Christ we have the constant help of God himself, living in us, abiding with us, directing us. In him, we have all the power and wisdom necessary to live a godly life of gospel freedom. Instead of memorizing 636 rules and striving to keep them, we only need to walk in the Spirit.

However, in some ways, this Spirit-led path is harder. Rule

keeping can be simpler, leaving less to our own conscience. Rule keeping is more objective, spelling out specific upright behaviors. Rule keeping encourages uniformity so that there are fewer conflicts between believers over lifestyle decisions. On the other hand, walking in the Spirit demands moment-by-moment attentiveness to his leading. It requires steady cooperation with him. It calls for constant choosing to side with him in the battle against the flesh.

🄷 WORD WEALTH

In its most basic meaning, *flesh* is meat, the soft tissue of any creature that can be stripped from bones. We see this meaning in John 1:14 and Hebrews 2:14 when the authors explain the incarnation of God the Son, who takes on a physical body to join the rest of humanity. After the resurrection, Jesus tells his disciples to touch him, "A spirit does not have a body of flesh and bone as you see that I have" (Luke 24:39). This basic meaning is also present in Revelation 19:21, when the carrion birds are called to eat the flesh of those killed in the final battle. This meaning is common enough. Sometimes flesh is just flesh.

However, sometimes *flesh* is a profound spiritual metaphor. When the New Testament writers mention flesh, they usually mean attitudes and motivations that are purely natural, physical, or fundamentally human, even sinful. Flesh in this light is generally opposed to things spiritually enlightened or supernatural. Flesh is almost always in contrast to the ways of God. When Peter is commended for recognizing Jesus' divinity, Jesus says, "This was not revealed to you by flesh and blood, but by my Father in heaven" (Matthew 16:17 NIV), drawing a distinction between what could be known naturally and what was revealed supernaturally. *Flesh* can refer to our entire status without supernatural regeneration by faith in Christ in the ways we think, the ways we behave, and the emotions and motivations that influence us. So this concept can also be translated as *the world*, *human standards*, *human reason*, or *sinful nature*. This is how Paul uses the term in Galatians.

New Fight

We all know the battle firsthand. We resolve to change a sinful habit. We plan to serve someone else in a practical way. We recognize and repent of an evil motive or attitude. We are certain that we will do better from now on.

But then, reality.

It turns out that the old habit has a firmer grip on us than we thought. We shrugged off that service opportunity because it was easier to stay home. That old attitude keeps surfacing before we notice. It seems we are helpless to live our new life in Christ. What is happening here?

We are engaged in an epic spiritual battle. When armies line up for battle, their leaders have specific goals in mind. Both sides want to defend the territory they already hold while taking new ground. This holds true for spiritual battles too. When any individual comes to faith in Christ, he comes with habits and instincts already formed. This territory belongs to the flesh and will not be surrendered easily. Upon conversion, the Spirit begins its relentless battle to transform the whole being into the character of Christ. This lifelong conflict proceeds unevenly as one area after another gradually gives ground to the Spirit.

Isn't it startling how God the Spirit can be opposed by our own stubborn nature? Omnipotent God opposed by our own desires? How is that an even fight? The humility of God is astounding! He could overpower us, forcing us to conform to his will, but he insists on our cooperation. He will not drive us to fight this spiritual campaign. He will lead and he will prompt. He will teach and correct. But he refuses to conquer the flesh without our cooperation.

So we must continually choose a side. We choose in every situation whether to cooperate with the flesh or the Spirit. The flesh is the path of least resistance, of course. The fleshly habits are what come naturally. Still, there is the opportunity at every juncture to side with the Spirit, to produce his fruit, and to win the battle.

To join in this battle, we must first have the Holy Spirit. Without him, there is no battle. There is no battle when we are living in our own strength by rules or social customs. We keep them or we fail to keep them through our own effort. Without the Spirit, there is no divine help to live the new life.

The Holy Spirit lives in those who belong to Christ by faith (Romans 8:9; 1 Corinthians 12:13). The person who has never heard the gospel, who has never turned to God in repentance, who has never trusted in Christ's provision for sin, who has never been made righteous through faith in him, that person is on his own. There is no Spirit in us to make war against our flesh.

- *Anyone can see the fruit of living in the flesh without the Spirit. What obvious fruit flows from that kind of living (Galatians 5:19–21)? While all the sins listed are fleshly, which ones are most easily associated with bodily desires? Which ones have more to do with sinful human nature?*

- *What are those individuals who produce this kind of fruit revealing about themselves (v. 21)? Are they the heirs of God that Paul described in Galatians 4?*

- *In contrast, what fruit grows from living in the Spirit (5:22–23)?*

- *These two lists are stark opposites. Take note that the "works of the flesh" (the self-life) are plural, but the fruit of the Spirit is singular. What does this indicate about living with or without the Spirit?*

- *Why can a Christian be confident that living by the Spirit pleases God (vv. 22–23)?*

- *Compare Galatians 5:24–25 to 2:20 and 5:16. What does it mean to crucify our flesh and live by the Spirit?*

- *When Paul completes his thought (5:26), what additional fruit of the flesh does he mention?*

New Fruit

Growing is a lot less work than we imagine. Leaves simply grow on a healthy tree. Fruit grows naturally on a healthy branch. It is tempting to look at a list like the one Paul supplies and ask, *How am I doing? What fruit am I lacking? How can I do better?* But that's not what Paul teaches here. His solution to fleshly fruit or sparse fruit is to get in step with the Spirit. The Christian who depends on the Spirit for *new* life also depends on the Spirit for *daily* life. Living in the Spirit *will* produce an abundance of the fruit of the Spirit.

⟨⟩ EXPERIENCE GOD'S HEART

- *Do you ever feel the spiritual battle raging in your life? Have you experienced spiritual victory? Describe your feelings when the Spirit wins. And when the flesh wins.*

- *Spiritual fruit grows in the life of people who live by the Spirit. What clear evidence is there that you are spiritually alive? What fruit listed in Galatians 5 is obvious to yourself and others?*

9 SHARE GOD'S HEART

- *Most Christians know someone who professes to be a Christian, but it is hard to see any evidence of the Holy Spirit's presence in their life. Maybe you know someone like that. Spend some time praying for that person.*

- *You also probably know someone who obviously demonstrates some of the fruit of the Spirit. Take note of something specific. Reach out to that person with an encouraging comment. For example, "At the school meeting, I saw you handle conflict with supernatural patience."*

Talking It Out

1. Look up these passages about the love ethic of the Christian gospel. Discuss with your group the implications of each. How is this way of love new? How does it govern the character and actions of Jesus' people? How does it free us?

Passage	Truths about the Love Ethic
Matthew 22:34–40	
John 13:34–35	
1 Corinthians 13:8–13	
Galatians 6:1–3	
1 John 2:3–11	
2 John 5–6	

2. Jesus taught his disciples about producing godly spiritual fruit. With your group, compare John 15:1–5 to Galatians 5:22–25. How did Jesus say we would produce much fruit? How did Paul say we live fruitful, godly lives?

LESSON 11

The Burdens We Bear

(Galatians 6:1–10)

Flying small aircraft is a wonderful experience that offers many benefits but involves many risks. Mother Nature, geography, airplane mechanics, human physiology, and the unexpected are just a few broad challenges that a pilot must constantly evaluate to determine whether he or she can accomplish a flight safely. The student pilot must learn how to face these challenges using all the skills and systems available.

To take an obvious example, knowing that the craft is a safe distance from the ground is life or death. Student pilots will learn to observe the altitude of the plane with their own eyesight. For a variety of reasons, ordinary observation may fail. Swift weather changes, cockpit distractions, or simple mistakes can confuse or mislead the pilot. At that point, secondary systems come into play. Gages, radar, global position maps, and audible alarms are some of the systems in place to back up the pilot's senses. Even with all this gear, a flustered new pilot can still make fatal mistakes, so in the second seat is a calm and more experienced pilot who can step in to correct a dangerous trajectory.

The point of all these redundant systems is survival. Each level of safety measures keeps the operator and aircraft from disaster. At any point, the new pilots know that they can make corrections and, ultimately, that they are not alone on the journey.

When a student pilot misses all the warnings and is heading

toward disaster, having a mature pilot alongside is literally a life-saver. Although instructors will occasionally take control of an aircraft, usually they calmly but urgently speak correction to the student. The instructors cannot step in every time. They do not want to do the flying for the new pilots. They want their students to succeed. They want the new pilots to fly on their own.

Wise instructors know how to give corrections without sapping the enthusiasm of their students. They can do this by keeping some simple things in mind. They can remember the times they needed correction themselves. They may wish they had had more patient copilots during their own training. They might acknowledge that they can still make unsafe decisions at times when a second pilot would be very helpful. This humble attitude gives more than correction to the student; it gives the confidence to carry on.

Spiritual Help

In Galatians 5:13–25, Paul explained several ways that Christians can live godly lives free from the obligations of the Mosaic law. He described some ways that we can win the constant battle between flesh and Spirit without the return to rule keeping that Judaizers were pushing. To avoid indulging our own fleshly desires, we should turn our attention to the needs of others. By living the love ethic that Jesus taught, we are freed to choose godly actions beyond what the law ever imagined. And with constant attention to the Holy Spirit's leading, we can keep in step with him and produce his good fruit.

However, we know from experience that even with all those "systems" as safeguards, we can still become trapped in sinful patterns that reflect the old life rather than the new. We can still gratify the desires of the flesh. A flustered, confused, or distracted Christian can make spiritually lethal mistakes. Thankfully, on this spiritual journey, we are not alone.

- *What can it mean for a Christian to be "caught" or "overtaken" in a sin or fault (Galatians 6:1)?*

- *When Christians are caught in a sin, who should help them? According to 5:16–25, what qualifies someone as a spiritual person?*

- *What is the goal of the helper in this situation? How must the helper approach this tricky situation?*

- *Why must the helper be careful? What attitude could lead to trouble for the helper?*

The word translated *caught* or *overtaken* does not connote being trapped and helpless to escape, like an animal caught in a snare.[28] It means literally *detected* or *surprised*, implying that the Christian in question here has been discovered committing sin. It means they were discovered committing some indulgence of the flesh (5:13), a failure to live the love ethic (v. 14), or an action clearly out of step with the Holy Spirit of God (v. 25). Perhaps in this situation, both parties are caught off-guard.

Taking Paul's instructions to heart in Galatians 5, we know that confronting sin is something we should do out of love and in step with the Spirit. Here in chapter 6, we see what that looks like. There is no place in the rebuke for harsh judgment, public shaming, blackmail, or rejection. Instead, the spiritual helper, under the direction of the Holy Spirit and full of the Spirit's fruit, restores the errant Christian to life in the Spirit.

- *What is the law of Christ (6:2; 5:14)? How does Paul say that we can fulfill the Anointed One's law?*

- *Based on the context of 6:2, what does carrying one another's troubles probably mean? Do you have fellow Christians who help you carry your troubles? Do you help to carry anyone else's troubles?*

Paul is talking about a burden that's a heavy weight carried over a great distance. This is not the swift feat of a weightlifter, not up and down and done. This is an oppressively heavy rock carried for miles for weeks on a winding uphill trek. Our long-term burdens can be practical needs, such as health challenges, difficult relationships, or financial shortages. In this context of addressing sin, it may be a specific temptation to sin and moral failure.

Whatever the struggle, we must recognize that instant deliverance is not always God's plan. The deliverance described here is slow and steady teamwork. It is the gradual transformation of a fleshly convert into a spiritual disciple with the continual restorative input of others. This process requires maturity as it builds maturity in both parties.

- *In the context of sin and the confronting of sin, how might Christian helpers deceive themselves (v. 3)?*

- *What should be a believer's focus (v. 4)?*

- *How does verse 5 compare with verse 2? How can we carry one another's troubles but still be responsible for our own consciences?*

Not every weight is an oppressive burden. Some weight-bearing is helpful. The fitness conscious seek out weights at the local gym to build their muscles and increase their stamina. This is the kind of load mentioned here, a temporary load like a box or a barrel being unloaded from a ship.

While we need help with the oppressive long-term burdens of life, we also need to take responsibility for the temporary loads we are called to bear. For the Christian to depend on others to carry these loads would permanently stunt his own maturity. This steady exercise of lifting and serving, of humble self-examination, is necessary to grow.

- *What connection do you see between the instructor (v. 6) and the situation of a Christian caught in a sin (v. 1)?*

- *What should we do for those who teach us in the Scriptures? Give some examples of good things we could share with them.*

There was a minister who spent almost forty years pastoring churches in western Canada. In those days, it was customary for churches to pay low wages to their leaders. Sometimes that was because it was all the church could afford. Sometimes it was out of the conviction that a pastor should serve "because he loves the Lord" and not for "filthy lucre" (see Titus 1:11 KJV). As a result, there were times when he took multiple jobs to supplement his meager income.

In one community, he was the bus driver and the grave digger while serving as the local pastor. One day, after delivering children to the school, he switched clothes, hurried to the cemetery, and dug a grave. He rushed home, took a shower, changed clothes again, and scurried back to the church for the funeral. After the graveside service, he dismissed the mourners, changed his clothes yet again, and filled in the grave. All without a complaint. It was his privilege to serve the Lord.

In another church, the wages were low, but the parishioners were farmers. At harvest, they filled his larder. On butchering day, they filled the freezer. His family had the use of the corner of a neighboring church member's field for a garden. This church, full of practical people, always seemed to be meeting a practical need for this pastor and his family. They shared what good things they had with their teacher.[29]

The status of Christian shepherds, whether volunteers, bi-vocational, or full-time, is unimportant, but this principle is important. When someone consistently delivers the spiritual, life-sustaining truth, it is reasonable and right to return this invaluable kindness with kindness of your own.

 DIGGING DEEPER

Jesus taught this to his disciples when he sent them out to minister. Paul taught this principle repeatedly in his letters—namely that the churches he founded should provide materially for their leaders. Ministers who teach you the love ethic ought to be loved in practical ways. If they help you carry your burden, you should help them carry theirs.

- *The passages listed in the following chart provide instructions and examples of this provision principle. Look up each passage and then note next to it what you learned.*

Passage	Provision Principle
Deuteronomy 24:14–15	
Luke 10:7	
Romans 15:25–27	
1 Corinthians 9:3–14	
1 Timothy 5:17–18	

Guaranteed Results

To conclude the ethical exhortation of his letter, Paul turns to a commonsense illustration. Imagine a farmer plowing his field, picking the large rocks out of it, digging furrows, planting seeds, protecting the field against bugs, and pulling weeds without any expectation of a harvest. Such a farmer would be ridiculous.

We do not plant seeds because we enjoy the outdoors. We do not plant seeds to discard them. We do not plant seeds to give them a proper burial. We do it because we expect something to grow from them. There is no other purpose. The reason for the sowing is the harvest.

- *State in your own words the principle of planting and reaping (Galatians 6:7–8).*

- *How does denying the reality of harvest mock God? How does it mock God when we expect no corruption when we sow to the flesh (the self-life)?*

• *What kind of seed produces corruption? What kind produces everlasting life?*

• *Look back at 5:16–23. How does this principle of sowing and reaping fit with that passage?*

 DIGGING DEEPER

"You reap what you sow."

"What goes around, comes around."

"Karma bites, dude."

Even our own society recognizes the truth of planting and reaping. Not only is this illustration commonsense, but it is also commonplace. But don't let the commonness of the idea obscure its profoundness. Can you imagine trying to live in a world where this wasn't the case? God designed our world with pragmatic, built-in predictability. The Bible uses this notion of planting and reaping many times in both the Old and New Testaments because it adheres so thoroughly to God's design.

Match the Scriptures on the right with the key phrases about sowing on the left. The first match has been made for you.

e	Fruit of righteousness will be peace, quietness, and confidence.	a.	Job 4:8
	Forgive and you will be forgiven. Give and it will be given to you.	b.	Psalm 126:5–6
	God's Word accomplishes its purpose.	c.	Proverbs 11:17–19
	Others have done the hard work. You will reap their harvest.	d.	Proverbs 22:8–9
	Peacemakers sow peace and reap righteousness.	e.	Isaiah 32:16–20
	Seed sprouts and grows without the farmer's help.	f.	Isaiah 55:10–11
	Sow injustice, reap calamity.	g.	Hosea 8:7
	Sown perishable, raised imperishable; sown in weakness, raised in power.	h.	Hosea 10:12–13
	Sow righteousness, reap reward.	i.	Matthew 13:18–23
	Sow righteousness, reap unfailing love.	j.	Mark 4:26–29
	Sow spiritual seed, reap material harvest.	k.	Luke 6:37–38
	Sow tears, reap joyful songs.	l.	John 4:35–38
	Sow the wind, reap the whirlwind.	m.	1 Corinthians 9:10–12
	Sow trouble and reap it.	n.	1 Corinthians 15:36–44
	Successful sowing depends on the soil.	o.	Galatians 6:7–9
	You reap what you sow.	p.	James 3:17–18

By the way, can you think of any important biblical idea that offers relief from this principle of harvest? Hint: It is the central theme of Galatians.

Patience for the Harvest

Every apple contains an orchard. Apples, like all other living things, are designed to reproduce after their kind; like produces like (Genesis 1). Within apples are what's needed to reproduce—namely, apple seeds. But these seeds will not produce an orchard tomorrow. That kind of harvest takes generations. Every apple holds many seeds, every seed is a potential tree, every tree is potential for more apples, and every apple holds many seeds, and so on. Getting from an apple to an orchard takes great patience and perseverance.

Spiritual harvest is a long-term prospect too. Every Christian has the Spirit and the love ethic for guidance. Every day of the Christian life holds many opportunities for sowing to the Spirit. All sowing to the Spirit reaps good spiritual fruit (Galatians). While that fruit grows, so do we. Spiritual maturity happens while we persevere.

- *What will be our harvest if we sow corrupt seeds (Galatians 6:8)?*

- *What will be our harvest if we plant "the good seeds of Spirit-life" (v. 8; cf. 5:22–23)?*

- *Can this spiritual work be exhausting? How? What should motivate us to continue these spiritual labors?*

- *When should we sow this spiritual seed (6:10)? Is there any specific group we should prioritize in our service to others?*

In this short passage, we have gone from getting caught in a sin to persevering in good deeds toward one another. In nearly every verse, it is clear we are not alone. We already learned that we have the Spirit in our lives if we have come to the Father through faith in Christ. Beyond that, we have Christian brothers and sisters to walk with us as we keep in step with the Spirit.

We need one another. We need each other to recover from tumbles with sin, to carry one another's burdens, to sow and harvest, to persevere and do good. The writer of Hebrews exhorted his readers with this same truth:

> Discover creative ways to encourage
> others and to motivate them toward acts
> of compassion, doing beautiful works as
> expressions of love. This is not the time to
> pull away and neglect meeting together, as
> some have formed the habit of doing. In

fact, we should come together even more frequently, eager to encourage and urge each other onward as we anticipate that day dawning. (Hebrews 10:24–25)

EXPERIENCE GOD'S HEART

- *Can you remember a moment you were caught in a sin or a significant fault? Without excuse. Ashamed. Even the remembrance is embarrassing. What follows in a moment like that makes all the difference. Was the response from others a severe scolding or further shaming? Was it shock or sadness or compassion? Which of these responses has the most potential for restoration? Why is this so?*

- *We are assured that there is a harvest ahead of us if we don't lose heart. Have you grown weary doing what is right? Why does this happen? What can encourage you to carry on?*

- *Has any other Christian ever helped you keep going? Describe this incident.*

❤ SHARE GOD'S HEART

- *This passage has an explicit assignment for those who are yielded to the Spirit. Have you caught someone in a sin? Our obligation of love to those in that predicament is to restore them. Unfortunately, there are many opportunities to carry out this assignment: gossip, pride, unkindness, lust, and rage among Christians, to name a few. Maybe you sense the Spirit's nudge to restore someone. Keep in step with him and do it.*

- *Because we want to obey Christ's love ethic, we can take steps to be restored when we fail. If there are believers you know who have your best interests in mind, who are spiritual and mature, talk to them about this. Tell them that you want them to correct and restore you when you need it.*

Talking It Out

1. With your small group, talk about the confrontations you have experienced. Talk about what sort of person is most effective in a rebuke and what sort of person makes you resistant. Are any of you that sort of person? If it suits the nature of your group, you could give one another explicit permission to confront you when it's necessary.

2. Read Hebrews 10:24–25 together and do it. Discuss what things you can do to motivate one another. Make a list of the things that motivate you all. Now that you know, what could keep you from meeting together on a regular basis? How can you help one another remain in community?

LESSON 12

Identifying with the Cross

(Galatians 6:11–18)

After years of daydreaming about it, City Slicker and City Slacker moved out west to buy a cattle ranch. Months later, their pal Pete came out for a visit. When he rolled down the long gravel driveway in his Jeep, Pete found Slicker and Slacker standing in an empty field. He climbed out and said hello. Then he asked, "How are things going, fellas?"

"Well enough," Slicker replied, "now that we've stopped quarreling."

"What was the quarrel about?" asked Pete.

"We couldn't settle on a name for the ranch," said Slacker. "He wanted Bar-8, and I wanted Lazy-H. Then we changed our minds, and he wanted Double-C, and I wanted Diamond-Arrow."

"How did you decide?" the friend inquired.

"We couldn't choose. So we named it the Bar-8-Lazy-H-Double-C-Diamond-Arrow Ranch," answered Slicker.

"Whew! That's enough of a name! Where are all your cattle, then?" puzzled Pete.

They both replied together, "None of them survived the branding."

On a cattle ranch, it's important to be able to identify the stock. The rancher needs to be able to count them and distinguish one breed from another, including his brand from that of others. He needs to know at a glance which ones belong to him. That's why many ranchers brand their animals.

That's also why retail chains have logos and trademarks. That's why football teams have jerseys and mascots. That's why important documents need signatures. All are unique identifiers for laying claim to something.

As Paul wraps up his urgent letter to the Galatians, he writes about the use and misuse of identifiers. Most importantly, he points them to the symbol that sets the true Christian gospel apart from counterfeits.

Letters on the Letter

- *What does Paul want his readers to notice about his handwriting (Galatians 6:11)? What do large letters imply? Why might he want them to recognize his handwriting?*

As was suggested in Galatians 4:13–15, Paul probably had a vision problem. When he recalled the affection of the Galatians for him in the early days of their acquaintance, he was emotionally moved. He remembered how his illness brought them together and how the Galatians would have given him their own eyes if they could have. So he writes in lettering large enough for him to see.

Some commentators also perceive earnestness here. Maybe he wrote his conclusion with large letters to underscore its importance. Still others think he may have taken up the pen at this point to finish the letter in his own hand after dictating the rest to a secretary. Any of these suggestions may be accurate.

Certainly, as Paul closes this difficult letter, he wants his readers to notice that he is writing it himself. This letter has his identifying mark on it.

Circling Back to Circumcision

No identifying mark held more cultural and religious significance for the Jew than circumcision. Every generation of baby boys inside the covenant people had to undergo this ceremonial wounding. Every generation of parents brought their sons to the priests for this mark.

This identifier has been an important element of the letter. Circumcision is mentioned eighteen times! It was central to the Galatian controversy. The terms of gentile justification before God had to be settled. Must gentiles also take this mark to join the covenant people of God? Paul made a clear and decisive argument denying this requirement for righteousness. As he ends his letter, he circles back to the issue.

- *Paul suggests three motivations for those pushing circumcision on these gentile Christians (6:12–13). What are they?*

- *How would gentile Christians getting circumcised be impressive to others (v. 12)? Who would boast in such ceremonial ritual-keeping (v. 13)?*

- *Why would promoting circumcision in the gentile church avoid persecution (v. 12)? Persecution from whom (see Acts 15:1–2)?*

- *The Judaizers demanded that the gentiles follow the law if they wanted to belong to God. How well did they keep the law themselves (Galatians 6:13)? Why doesn't this inconsistency seem to bother them?*

Apparently, the Judaizers were on a mission to circumcise as many gentile Christians as they could. Like evangelists counting commitment cards or sinners' prayers uttered, with circumcision, they had a tangible measure of their success. This would impress other Judaizers, and they could revel in their successes together. They could brag about how many converts took the mark required in the law.

The Singular Symbol

- *Unlike his critics, Paul limits his boasting to some redemptive facts. What are they (Galatians 6:14)? What real-world symbol does he raise up to fully identify with Jesus?*

- *To what was Paul crucified (v. 14)?*

- *What is the only tangible thing that measures the progress of the gospel in a person's life (v. 15)? What is new about those in Christ (2 Corinthians 5:17)?*

The basis of the gospel is in that symbol: Christ, the Son of God, on a cross, dying for the sins of the world. Through that supreme act of love, he identified with every sinner and bore our sin to its just consequence.

In the profound moment of the cross, God's victory over the world and its demonic powers was complete. The "hostile spirits" of this world (Galatians 4:3; cf. Colossians 2:8, 20) and the "weak and feeble principles of religion" (Galatians 4:9) were crucified and completely undone. They have lost their power over us who identify with Christ.

And, as surely as Christ died in our place, we died with him. In that great exchange, our sin became his, and his righteousness became ours (2:19–20). We are dead to the flesh and alive to the Spirit (5:16–18). We are forever free from sin, living Christ's new life as his new creation.

In the light of Jesus' crucifixion and its implications for us, the number of circumcised or uncircumcised is a trivial matter (6:15). Only a shallow religionist could cherish such a superficial symbol over the cross.

 # THE BACKSTORY

Does Paul boast? In the following passages, he certainly makes lists of his accomplishments, all the while denigrating them as nothing praiseworthy. Sometimes he feels compelled to give his extensive credentials. Ultimately, as here in Galatians, he boasts in the Lord (see 1 Corinthians 1:27–31; 9:13–18; 2 Corinthians 1:12–14; 10:7–18; 11:5–15, 16–30; 12:1–10; Philippians 3:2–11). What Paul does fits with what the Lord said through the prophet Jeremiah: "Let not the wise boast of their wisdom or the strong boast of their strength or the rich boast of their riches, but let the one who boasts boast about this: that they have the understanding to know me, that I am the LORD, who exercises kindness, justice and righteousness on earth, for in these I delight" (Jeremiah 9:23–24 NIV). Now that's something to boast about!

 THE EXTRA MILE

The transformation in store for us is total. As we deny the flesh and submit to the Spirit, we live a new life. This is not just the reformation of a bad character; it is the birth of a new person. This is not recycling; it is regeneration.

- *Look up the following passages to see the breadth of the newness that God has in mind as he redeems us and the whole world.*

	What's New?
Psalm 40:3	
Psalm 98:1	
Isaiah 42:9	
Isaiah 43:19	
Isaiah 62:2	
Isaiah 65:17	
Jeremiah 31:31	
Lamentations 3:22–23	
Ezekiel 36:26–27	

Matthew 13:52	
Mark 1:27	
Luke 5:36–39	
John 13:34	
Romans 6:4–5	
Romans 7:6	
1 Corinthians 11:25	
2 Corinthians 3:6	
Ephesians 2:15	
Colossians 3:10–11	
1 Peter 1:3–4	
Revelation 21:1–2	
Revelation 21:5	

Peaceful Parting

- *As he closes out his letter, who does Paul say will enjoy "true peace and God's delight" (Galatians 6:16)?*

- *Historically, who is part of Israel (6:16)? According to the argument of the whole letter to the Galatians, who are the offspring of Abraham now (3:7, 9, 29)?*

Surely, Paul knew that some of his readers would not receive his apostolic rebuke. Some of his readers might be the Judaizers themselves. There would be some gentile believers who had already been circumcised and submissive to the law, who were already too deceived to turn back. Others might be seeking confirmation from the local false teachers rather than the distant Paul.

However, there would also be some who were receptive and repentant. Paul singles them out for his statement about what blessing they will receive from God if they choose to live according to the true gospel.

Marks of a Martyr

Having suffered the undeserved criticism of the Judaizers, Paul demands that the Galatians stop entertaining their nonsense. Like the Master himself, who showed the signs of his sacrifice to the doubting disciples (Luke 24:37–43), Paul draws their attention to his own scars (Galatians 6:17).

Remember, when he first met the Galatians, they weren't all open to his preaching. Some of them were downright hostile, stoning him, dragging him outside the city, and leaving him for dead (Acts 14:19–20). Surely, being pelted with rocks until his body lay lifeless on the ground would have left some marks. These are probably the marks that identify Paul with Jesus. They may have come at the hands of his enemies, but Paul got them while representing Christ.

It is likely that, in addressing his ongoing persecution, he was graphically reminding them of the first persecution he received at their hands. It is as though he is asking, "Haven't I endured enough from you? Let's be done with it now."

Gracious Goodbye

- *Finally, Paul offers a general blessing to all his believing readers. Is there warmth at the end of this harsh, corrective letter? What does he wish for all the Galatians (Galatians 6:18)?*

- *How does this blessing fit with the rest of the letter?*

Paul concludes the way he began, with grace. The unmerited favor of God in Christ has been his theme throughout. A resilient understanding of God's grace is what he called them back to with this letter. All human effort, all ceremonial rites, and all good behavior will fall short. Only the grace of God can save, keep, and transform the true follower of Jesus Christ.

🔮 EXPERIENCE GOD'S HEART

- *The false teachers were measuring the Galatians' faith by outward standards. What are the dangers of doing that?*

- *Have you been misjudged because you didn't measure up to some extra-biblical demand? If so, what was it? How did this false judgment make you feel? How did you handle it?*

- *Have you misjudged others because they didn't measure up to some extra-biblical standard you placed on them? How did they receive what you said? What did your misjudgment do to your own soul? How did it affect your relationships?*

- *How has your understanding of grace changed as you worked your way through this Galatians study? For example, have you had to adjust your beliefs about salvation, righteousness, or freedom? If so, what adjustments have you made? Are you confident, based on what you have learned, that you are a child of God by his grace? If so, spend some time praising God for all he has done for you, for what he's doing now in you, and for what he has in store for you still.*

🌑 SHARE GOD'S HEART

One way we identify with Jesus is to worship with a body of Christians who boast in the cross. In worship, we can enthusiastically sing the truths of the gospel with and to one another. As we learn and practice the Scripture taught there, we will identify more and more with Christ. When we build relationships there, our fellowship of the cross grows deeper. Participating in a local church like that is the best way to consistently share God's heart.

- *Are you part of such a community of believers? If not, why? If you are, how are you living the gospel in their midst?*

- *When you belong to such a Christian community, invite someone to join you there. Many people have never experienced a living faith like that, so don't be afraid to invite them in.*

Talking It Out

1. Discuss ways that Christian leaders boast about their followers today. Can it be obvious or subtle? When do you notice it?

2. Do you ever boast about your own church? If so, what do you highlight to others?

3. What would change if our boasting were only in the cross?

4. Since Paul commends boasting in the cross, talk about how we can do this together as a group. What practices can we do together to boast in the cross? What activities can we do in the larger community that boast in the cross? What response should we pray for and expect as we magnify what Christ has done for us?

§

Appendix

Answer Key to Lesson 3 Timeline

The following dates for the ministry of Paul, including the letter to the Galatians, are all approximate and assume an early date for the writing of Galatians.

Acts	Galatians	Event or era leading to Jerusalem council	30	35	40	45	50
		Jesus' death, resurrection, and ascension	●				
8:1–3; 9:1–2	1:13–14	Saul persecutes the church	●				
9:3–19	1:15–16a	Saul's conversion	●				
	1:16–17	Paul taught by Jesus by revelation	●				
9:19–22	1:17	Paul's early preaching in Arabia and Damascus	●				
9:26–29	1:18–20	Paul's first visit to Jerusalem		●			

Acts	Galatians	Event or era leading to Jerusalem council	30	35	40	45	50
	1:21	Paul's ministry in Syria and Cilicia;					
10:1–11:18		Peter preaches gospel to the gentiles;		▬▬▬▬▬▬			
11:19–24		Gospel received by gentiles in Antioch					
	1:22–2:10	Paul's second visit to Jerusalem				•	
11:25–26		Barnabas and Paul minister in Antioch				●	
11:27–30		Famine in Judea; collection and delivery of gifts to Jerusalem				•	
13:1–14:25		First missionary journey among the Galatians				●	
14:26–28		Return to Antioch					
	2:11–16	Confrontation with Peter					•
		Galatians written					•
15:1–6		Jerusalem Council					•

Endnotes

1. Brian Simmons et al., "A Note to Readers," *The Passion Translation: The New Testament with Psalms, Proverbs, and Song of Songs* (Savage, MN: BroadStreet Publishing Group, 2020), ix.

2. The arguments for dating the Galatians letter are tied up with the epistle's recipients (North or South Galatia) and where one dates some of Paul's missionary activities. An excellent overview of the different viewpoints and the reasons provided for them can be found in Donald Guthrie's book *New Testament Introduction*, 4th ed. (Downers Grove, IL: InterVarsity Press, 1990), chap. 11. Another well done treatment of the issues is provided by Greg Herrick, "The Date and Destination of Galatians," Bible.org, June 28, 2004, https://bible.org/article/date-and-destination-galatians.

3. Martin Luther, *Luther's Works: The Sermon on the Mount and the Magnificat*, vol. 21, ed. Jaroslav Pelikan (St. Louis, MO: Concordia, 1956), 1100.

4. J. P. Moreland, as quoted in *The Case for Christ*, by Lee Strobel (Grand Rapids, MI: Zondervan, 1998), 249.

5   Moreland, as quoted in *The Case for Christ*, 248–49.

6   Timothy George, *Galatians* (Nashville, TN: Broadman & Holman Publishing, 1994), 191–2.

7   Brian Simmons et al., *The Passion Translation: The New Testament with Psalms, Proverbs, and Song of Songs* (Savage, MN: BroadStreet Publishing Group, 2020), Galatians 3:1, note 'c.'

8   If you would like to learn more about God's salvation plan for the world and how it has been going, here are some informative resources: John Piper, *Let the Nations Be Glad!* (Grand Rapids, MI: Baker Academic, 2022); Christopher J. H. Wright, *The Mission of God: Unlocking the Bible's Grand Narrative* (Downers Grove, IL: IVP Academic, 2018); Ruth A. Tucker, *From Jerusalem to Irian Jaya: A Biographical History of Christian Missions* (Grand Rapids, MI: Zondervan, 2004); Ralph Winter and Stephen C. Hawthorne, ed., *Perspectives on the World Christian Movement: A Reader*, 4th ed. (Pasadena, CA: William Carey Library, 2009); and Philip Jenkins, *The Next Christendom: The Coming of Global Christianity*, 3rd ed. (New York: Oxford University Press, 2011).

9   Lawrence P. Jacks, "A Good Word for Our Present Social System," *The Hibbet Journal* XXII.3 (April 22, 1924): 417.

10   Fanny Crosby, "Redeemed, How I Love to Proclaim It," 1882, public domain.

11   There are many excellent apologetic resources for explaining and defending Jesus' good news and the many other teachings of the Christian faith. Here are just a few of them: Francis Beckwith, William Lane Craig, and J. P. Moreland, eds., *To Everyone an Answer: A Case for the Christian Worldview* (Downers Grove, IL: IVP Academic, 2004); R. C. Sproul, *Defending Your Faith: An Introduction to Apologetics* (Wheaton, IL: Crossway, 2018); Gregory Koukl and Lee Strobel, *Tactics: A Game Plan for Discussing Your Christian Convictions* (Grand Rapids, MI: Zondervan, 2009); Norman L. Geisler, *The Big Book of Christian Apologetics: An A to Z Guide* (Grand Rapids, MI: Baker Books, 2012); Josh and Sean McDowell, *Evidence That Demands a Verdict: Life-Changing Truth for a Skeptical World* (Nashville, TN: Thomas Nelson, 2017); Lee Strobel, *The Case for Faith: A Journalist Investigates the Toughest Objections to Christianity* (Grand Rapids, MI: Zondervan, 2000); and J. Warner Wallace, *Cold-Case Christianity: A Homicide Detective Investigates the Claims of the Gospels* (Colorado Springs, CO: David C. Cook, 2013). Some excellent web sources are apologetics315.com, garyhabermas.com, and ngim.org.

12   Various Bible scholars date the composition of the New
      Testament books differently, with an increasing number
      of scholars concluding that the evidence points to all the
      books being completed by or just before AD 70, while
      others still consider some of the books to have been
      composed in the 90s. Many liberal Bible scholars even
      placed some of the books in the 120s and 130s. The
      most important argument for the earlier date is that the
      fulfillment of Jesus' prediction that the Jerusalem temple
      would be utterly destroyed (Matthew 24:1–2; Mark 13:1–2)
      occurred in 70 at the hands of the Romans, but none
      of the other New Testament books, such as the epistles,
      mention this prophecy coming to pass. Their silence on
      this fulfillment is a strong indication that the event had not
      yet occurred, for, the assumption is, if it had happened,
      the writers would have mentioned it and even made it
      part of their case that Jesus was the true Messiah. Critical
      Bible scholar John A. T. Robinson found this silence
      so strange and remarkable that it led him to seriously
      reconsider liberal late dates for the New Testament books.
      He published his findings in his book *Redating the New
      Testament* (Philadelphia, PA: Westminster Press, 1976), in
      which he argued that all the New Testament books were
      written by late 68, certainly before 70.

13   This position is held by many groups to some degree or other, but it is epitomized by the Hebrew Roots Movement. A diffuse movement with no centralized leadership, it can be difficult to delineate its ideology, but for a taste of this teaching, have a glance at websites like these and assess how their teachings square with what Paul says in Galatians: https://hebrewroots.info/what-is-the-hebrew-roots-movement/; https://davidwilber.com/articles/jesus-fulfilled-the-torah-what-does-that-mean; https://www.tabletmag.com/sections/belief/articles/observing-torah-like-jesus.

14   George, *Galatians*, 256.

15   E. P. Sanders, *Paul, the Law and the Jewish People* (Philadelphia, PA: Fortress Press, 1983), 68.

16   "Brothers Living in Cave Set to Inherit Share of Grandmother's £4Billion Fortune," *Daily Mail*, December 13, 2009, https://www.dailymail.co.uk/news/article-1235256/Brothers-living-cave-set-inherit-share-grandmothers-4billion-fortune.html.

17   See Cyril of Jerusalem, *On the Mysteries, II: Of Baptism (Lecture XX)*, Patristics, https://patristics.info/cyril-of-jerusalem-on-the-mysteries-ii-of-baptism.html; and Hippolytus, *The Apostolic Tradition*, Baptism, 21, https://www.gutenberg.org/files/61614/61614-h/61614-h.htm#teh21.

18   Irenaeus, *Against Heresies*, bk. III, chap. 19, New Advent, https://www.newadvent.org/fathers/0103319.htm.

19   C. S. Lewis, *Mere Christianity* (New York: Macmillan, 1952), 139.

20   Mark Griffiths, "The Psychology of New Year's Resolutions," The Conversation US, Inc., January 1, 2016, https://theconversation.com/the-psychology-of-new-years-resolutions-51847.

21   The thorn-in-the-flesh episode of 2 Corinthians 12:7–10 may be the only other reference to any illness of Paul, although scholars debate whether that was a physical or spiritual hardship.

22   This dog tale comes from the study guide writer, Matthew Boardwell, who is currently a missionary in Ireland.

23   C. K. Barrett, *Essays on Paul* (Philadelphia, PA: Westminster Press, 1982), 154–70; George, *Galatians*, 334.

24   For example, the following ministries have online resources telling the stories of Christians around the world who pay a severe price for following Jesus. They also issue quarterly print editions: Open Doors, PO Box 6, Witney, Oxon, OX29 6WG (www.opendoorsuk.org); Church in Chains, PO Box 10447, Glenageary, Dublin, Ireland (www.churchinchains.ie); The Voice of the Martyrs, 1815 SE Bison Rd., Bartlesville, OK 74006 (www.persecution.com). Additionally, Voice of the Martyrs, along with the Christian rock group DC Talk, published *Jesus Freaks*, Volumes 1 and 2 (Bloomington, MN: Bethany House, 1999, 2003). These are collections of short, readable, and inspiring Christian persecution stories, both ancient and contemporary.

25   Jeepster Gal of Rustic Colorado Photography has posted a seven-and-a-half minute video of this drive online. You can view it at https://www.youtube.com/watch?v=0oxMGAawrHE&ab_channel=JeepsterGal.

26   There are many parallels between Paul's letters to the Galatians and the Romans. Romans seems to be a more deliberate, less crisis-driven exposition of the same themes. Like Galatians, Romans highlights the similarities between Jews and gentiles in their need for justification by faith and apart from the works of the law. Romans also draws its conclusions from the life story and faith example of Abraham. So Romans asks this practical righteousness question after making essentially the same argument as Galatians. In both letters, this dilemma comes to the forefront as Paul turns from the theology of the gospel to its ethical implications.

27   A fascinating and insightful articulation and application of the Christian love ethic is provided by Norman L. Geisler in his book *The Christian Ethic of Love* (Grand Rapids, MI: Zondervan, 1973).

28   There are other passages specifically about being ensnared by sin. See Romans 7:14–25; Ephesians 4:20–24; 1 Timothy 6:6–10; 2 Timothy 2:24–26; Hebrews 12:1–2.

29   This pastor was the father-in-law of Matthew Boardwell, the writer of this study guide.

MY THOUGHTS

MY THOUGHTS

MY THOUGHTS

MY THOUGHTS

MY THOUGHTS

MY THOUGHTS